EASY GUITAR WITH NOTES & TAB

BOHEMIAN
RHAPSODY

MUSIC FROM THE MOTION PICTURE SOUNDTRACK

ISBN 978-1-5400-4680-2

Visit Hal Leonard Online at
www.halleonard.com

Contact us:
Hal Leonard
7777 West Bluemound Road
Milwaukee, WI 53213
Email: info@halleonard.com

In Europe, contact:
Hal Leonard Europe Limited
42 Wigmore Street
Marylebone, London, W1U 2RN
Email: info@halleonardeurope.com

In Australia, contact:
Hal Leonard Australia Pty. Ltd.
4 Lentara Court
Cheltenham, Victoria, 3192 Australia
Email: info@halleonard.com.au

STRUM AND PICK PATTERNS

This chart contains the suggested strum and pick patterns that are referred to by number at the beginning
of each song in this book. The symbols ⊓ and ∨ in the strum patterns refer to down and up strokes, respectively.
The letters in the pick patterns indicate which right-hand fingers play which strings.

p = thumb
i = index finger
m = middle finger
a = ring finger

For example; Pick Pattern 2
is played: thumb - index - middle - ring

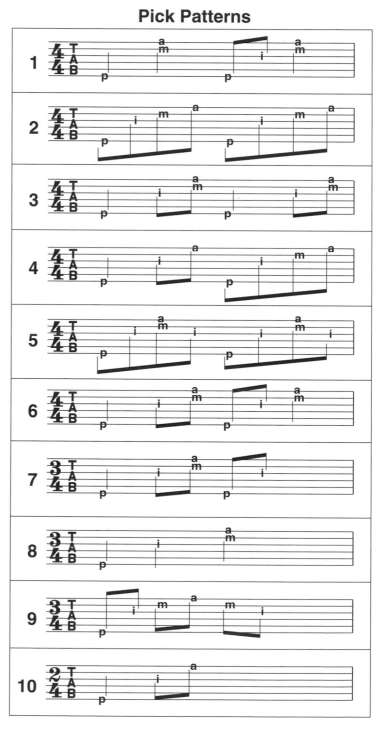

You can use the 3/4 Strum and Pick Patterns in songs written in compound meter (6/8, 9/8, 12/8, etc.).
For example, you can accompany a song in 6/8 by playing the 3/4 pattern twice in each measure.
The 4/4 Strum and Pick Patterns can be used for songs written in cut time (¢) by doubling the note
time values in the patterns. Each pattern would therefore last two measures in cut time.

Twentieth Century Fox Trademark

Composed by Alfred Newman

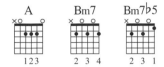

Strum Pattern: 4
Pick Pattern: 4

Moderately

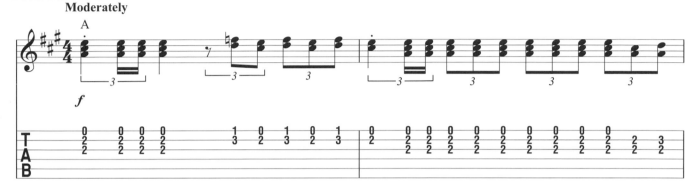

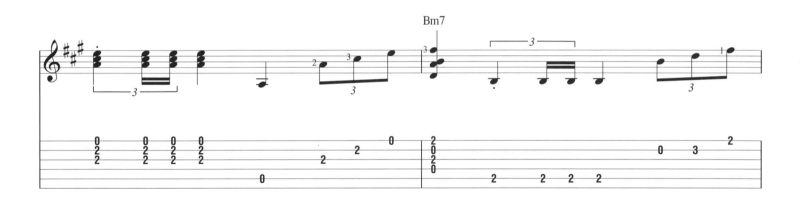

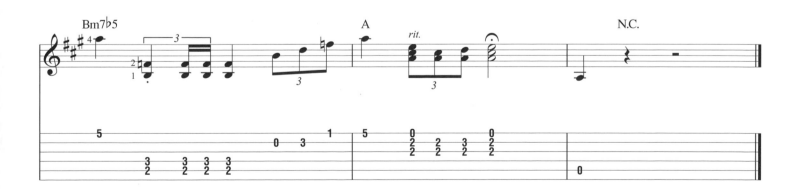

Somebody to Love

Words and Music by Freddie Mercury

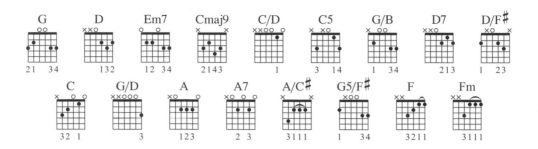

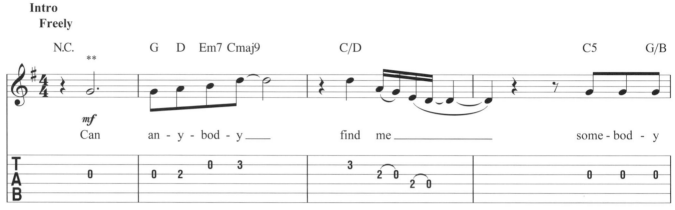

*Capo I

Intro
Freely

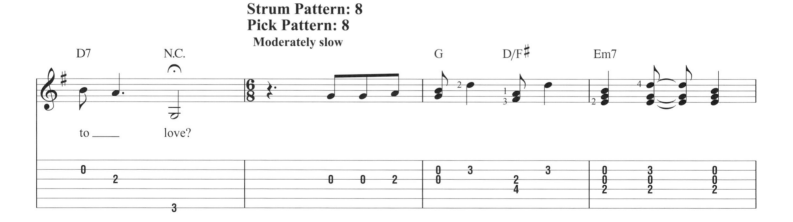

Can an-y-bod-y ___ find me ___ some-bod-y

*Optional: To match recording, place capo at 1st fret.

**Sung one octave higher through Intro.

Strum Pattern: 8
Pick Pattern: 8
Moderately slow

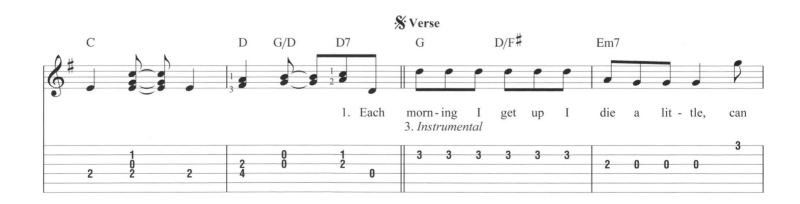

to ___ love?

% Verse

1. Each morn-ing I get up I die a lit-tle, can
3. *Instrumental*

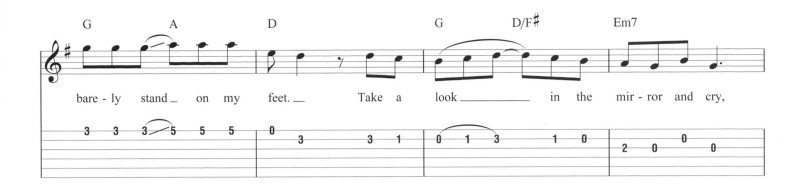

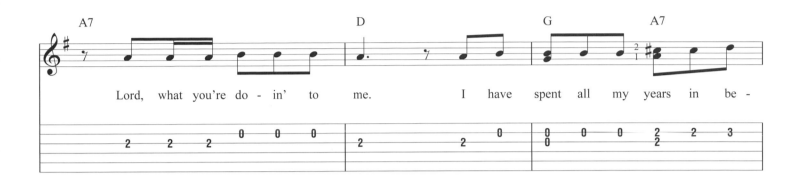

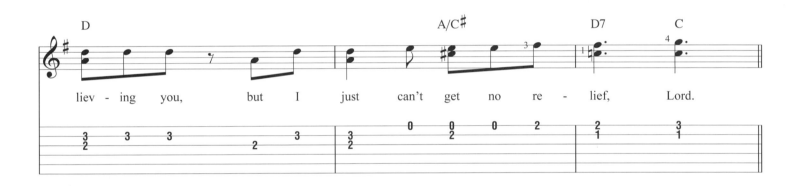

Chorus

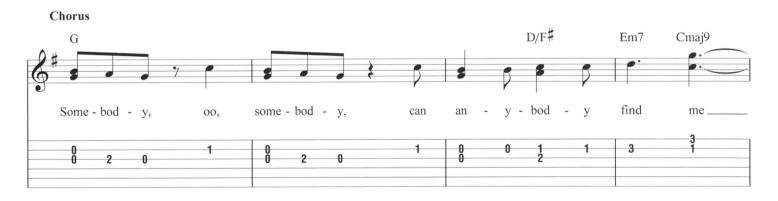

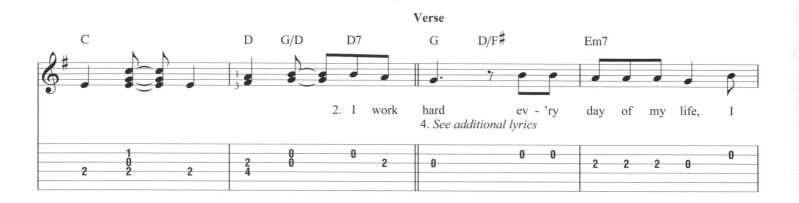

4. *See additional lyrics*

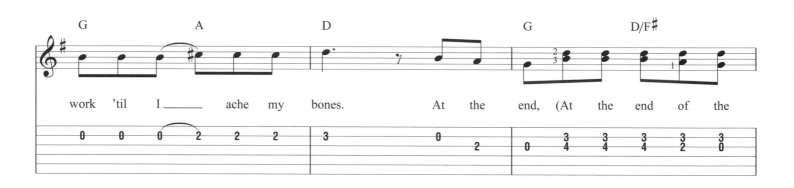

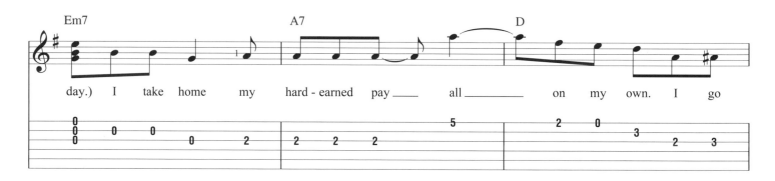

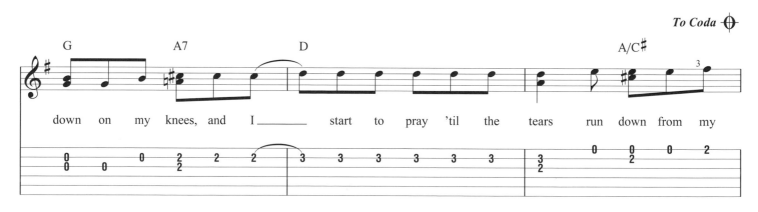

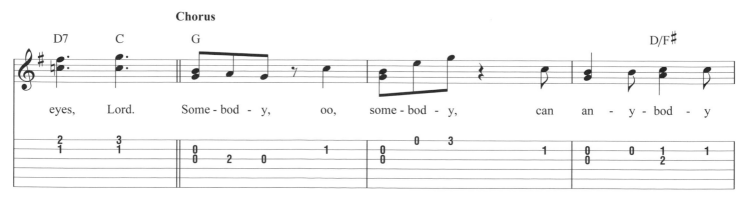

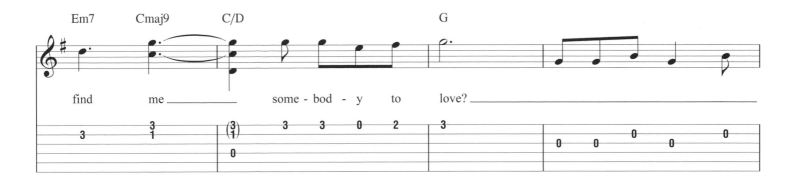

find me _____ some - bod - y to love? _____

Bridge

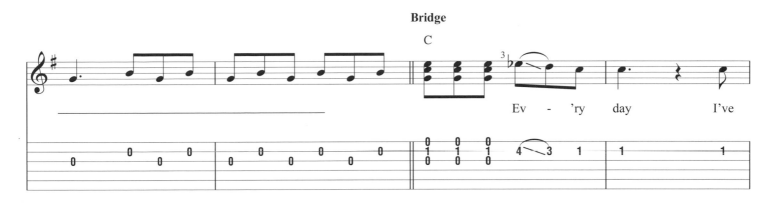

Ev - 'ry day I've

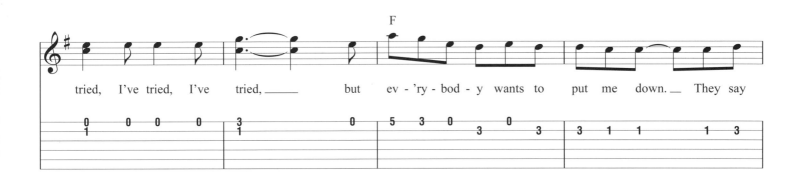

tried, I've tried, I've tried, _____ but ev - 'ry - bod - y wants to put me down. ___ They say

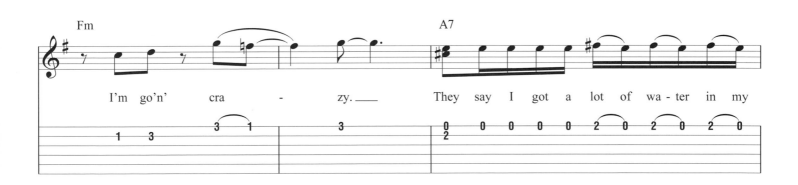

I'm go'n' cra - zy. ___ They say I got a lot of wa - ter in my

brain. I _____ got no com - mon sense, I got no - bod - y left to be -

lieve. _____

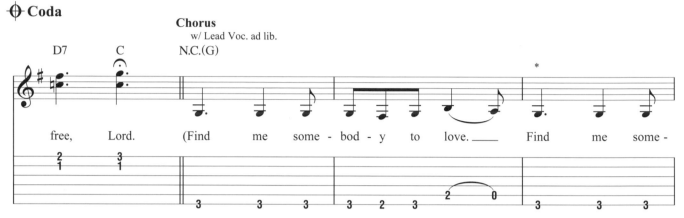

Coda

Chorus
w/ Lead Voc. ad lib.

free, Lord. (Find me some-bod-y to love. _____ Find me some-

*Sung one octave higher till end, except where noted.

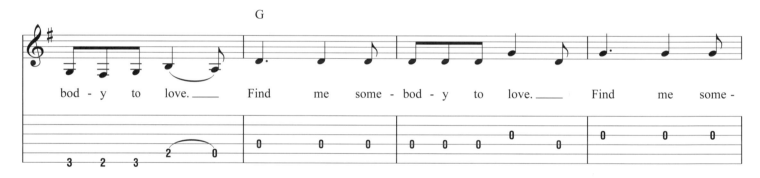

bod - y to love. _____ Find me some-bod-y to love. _____ Find me some-

bod - y to love. _____ Find me, me, some-bod-y to love. _____

bod - y to love. _____ Find me, me, some-bod-y to love. _____

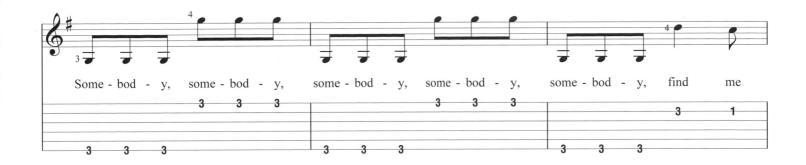

Some - bod - y, some - bod - y, some - bod - y, some - bod - y, some - bod - y, find me

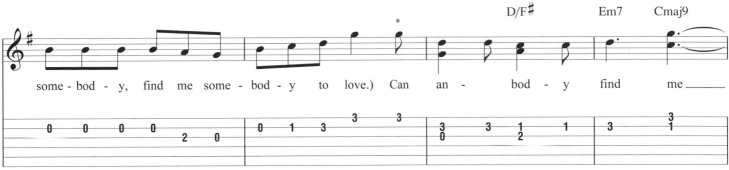

D/F#   Em7   Cmaj9

some - bod - y, find me some - bod - y to love.) Can an - bod - y find me _____

*Sung as written, next 6 meas.

Freely

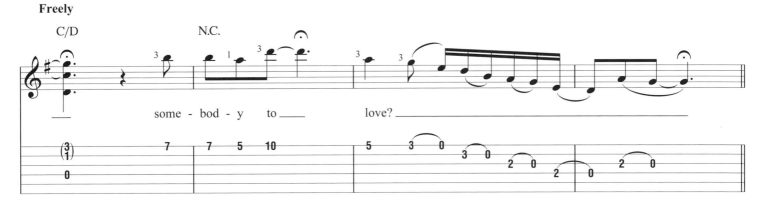

C/D   N.C.

some - bod - y to _____ love? _____

Outro
w/ Lead Voc. ad lib.

A Tempo   *Repeat and fade*

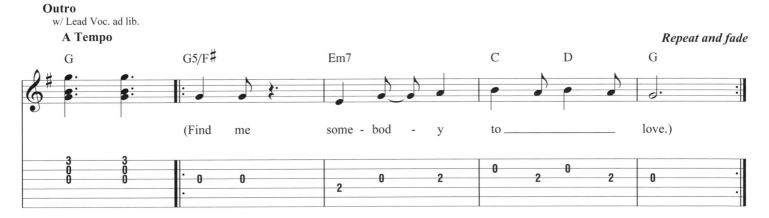

G   G5/F#   Em7   C   D   G

(Find me some - bod - y to _____ love.)

Additional Lyrics

4. Got no feel, I got no rhythm,
   I'll just keep losing my beat.
   I'm O.K., I'm alright.
   I ain't gonna face no defeat.
   I just gotta get out of this prison cell,
   Someday I'm gonna be free, Lord.

Doing All Right

Words and Music by Brian May and Tim Staffell

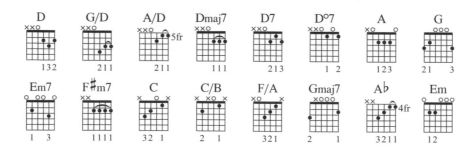

*Capo II

Strum Pattern: 1, 2

Pick Pattern: 5, 2

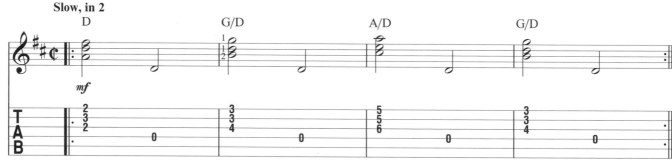

*Optional: To match recording, place capo at 2nd fret.

1., 3. Yes - ter - day ___ my life was ___ in ru - in.

2. *See additional lyrics*

Now to - day ___ { I know } { God knows } what I'm do - in'.

Got a feel - in' I should ___ be do - in' ___ all

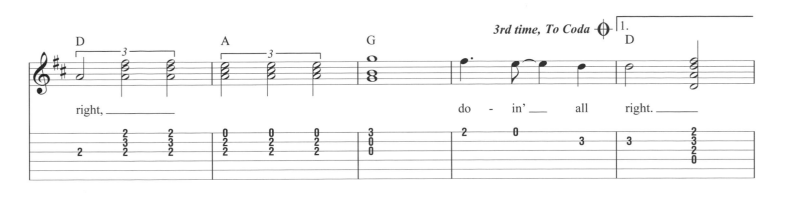

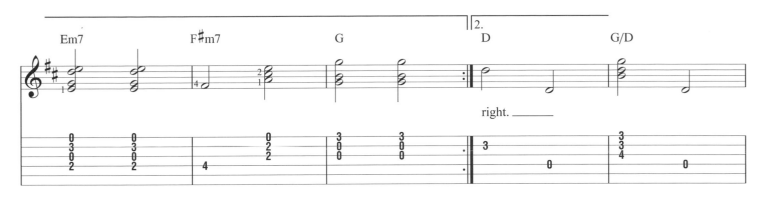

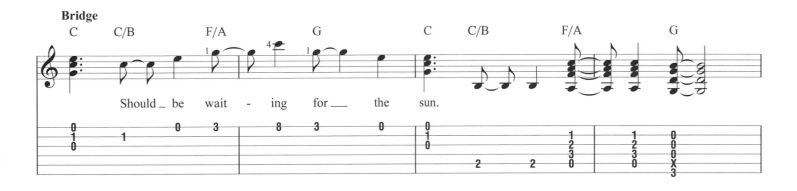

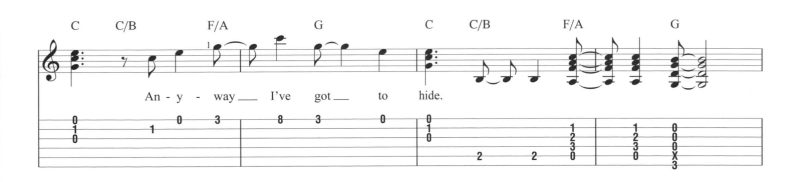

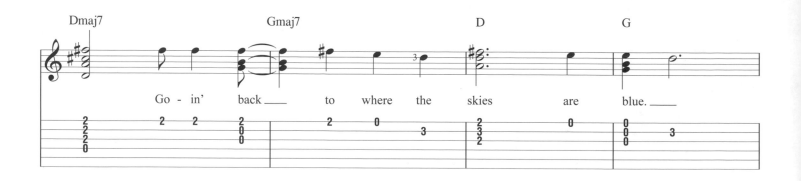

Go - in' back ____ to where the skies are blue. ____

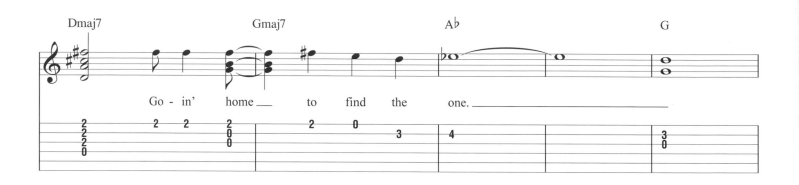

Go - in' home ____ to find the one. _____

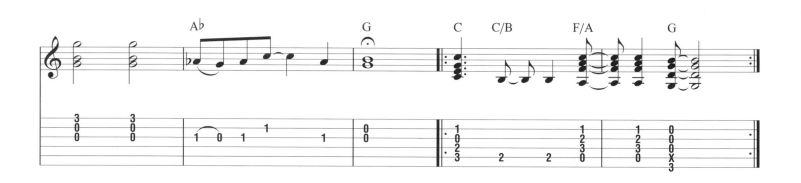

Should __ be wait - ing for ____ the sun. _____

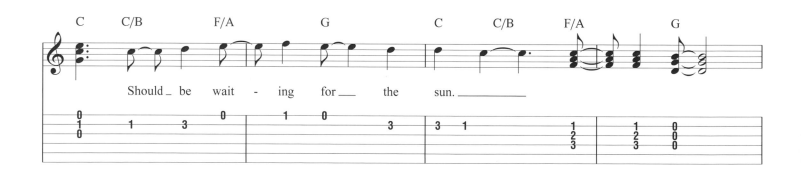

But an - y - way ____ I've got to hide _____ a - way.

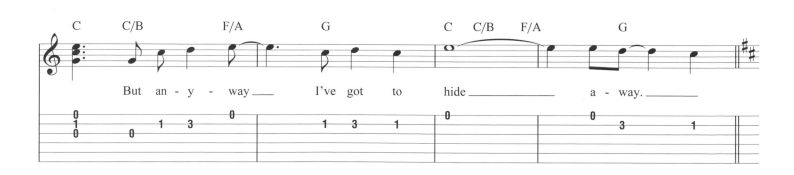

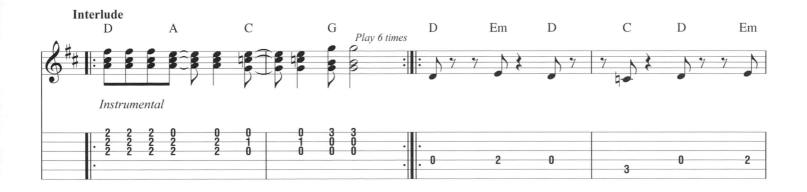

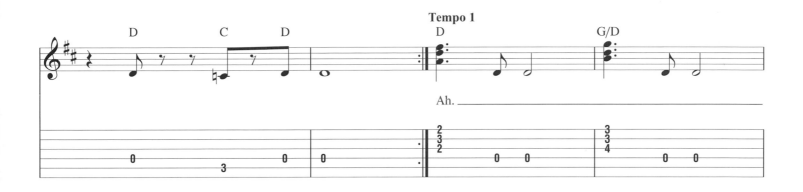

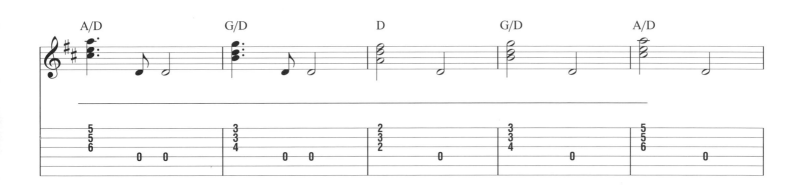

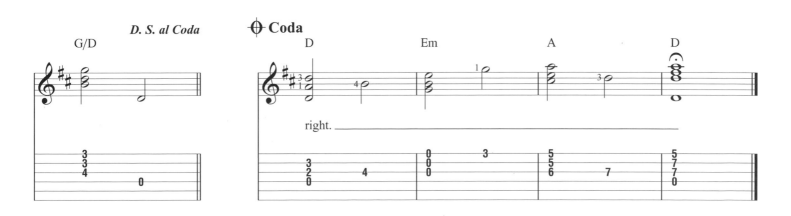

Additional Lyrics

2. Where will I be this time tomorrow?
   Jumped in joy or sinkin' in sorrow?
   Anyway, I should be doin' all right,
   Doin' all right.

Keep Yourself Alive

Words and Music by Brian May

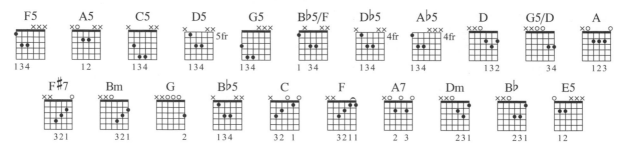

Strum Pattern: 3
Pick Pattern: 1

Intro
Moderately fast

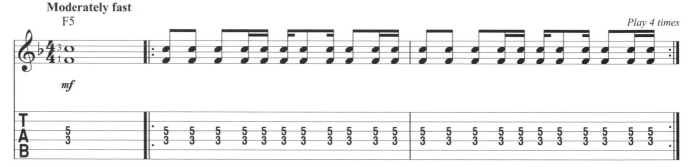

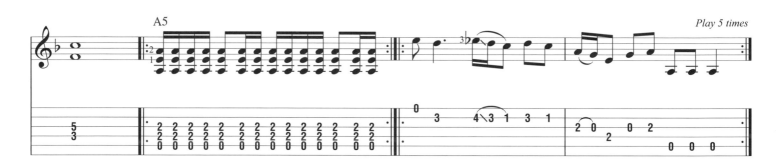

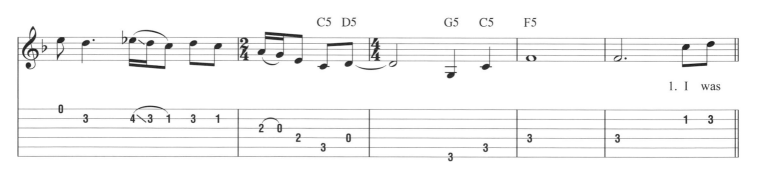

1. I was

told a mil-lion times of all the trou-bles in my way, mind you grow a lit-tle wis-er, lit-tle
loved a mil-lion wom-en in a bel-la-don-nie haze, and I ate a mil-lion din-ners brought to

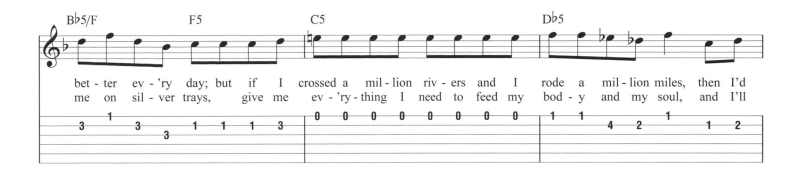

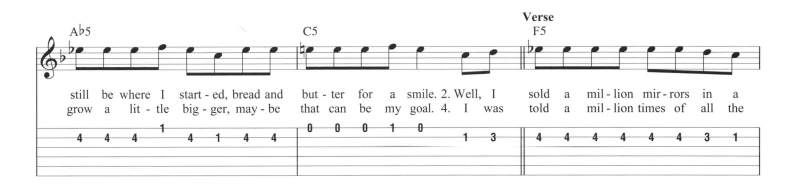

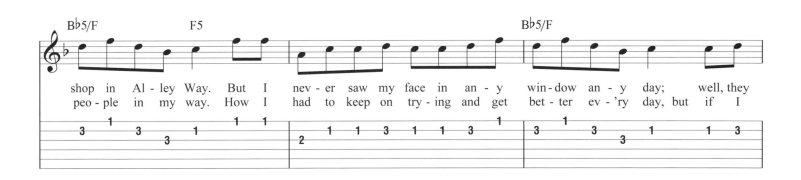

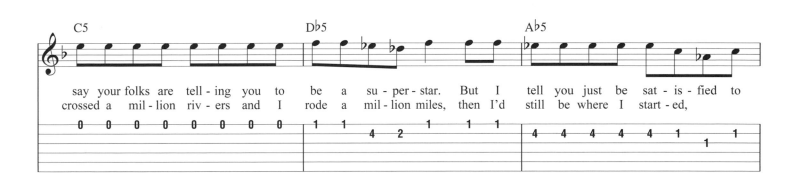

better ev-'ry day? No,___ I just think I'm two steps near-er to my grave.___

Chorus

Keep your-self a - live. Keep your-self a - live.___

Chorus

All you peo - ple, keep your-self a - live. Keep your-self a - live. Keep your-self a - live.___

Outro-Chorus

All you peo - ple, keep your - self a - live. Keep your - self a - live.

Keep your-self a - live. All you peo - ple, keep your-self a - live.

Killer Queen

Words and Music by Freddie Mercury

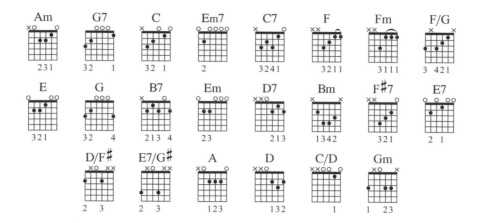

*Capo III

Strum Pattern: 3, 4
Pick Pattern: 1, 3

𝄋 **Verse**

Moderately

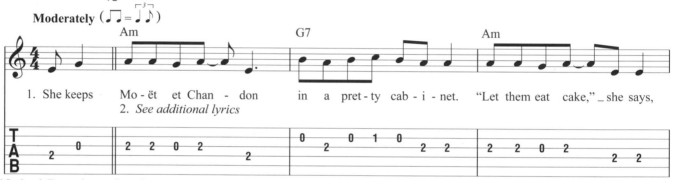

1. She keeps Mo-ët et Chan-don in a pret-ty cab-i-net. "Let them eat cake," she says,
2. *See additional lyrics*

*Optional: To match recording, place capo at 3rd fret.

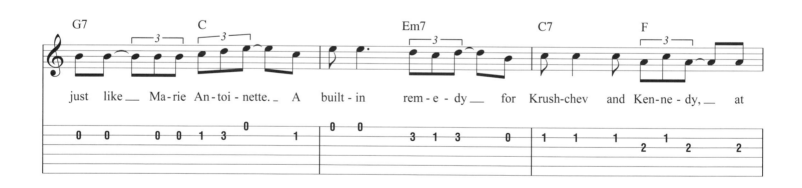

just like Ma-rie An-toi-nette. A built-in rem-e-dy for Krush-chev and Ken-ne-dy, at

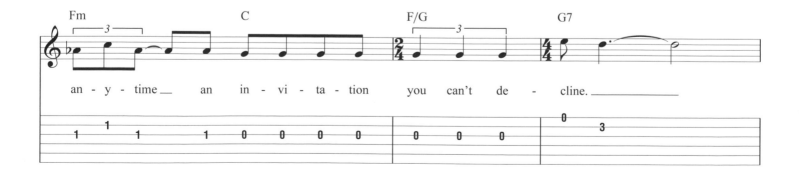

an-y-time an in-vi-ta-tion you can't de-cline.

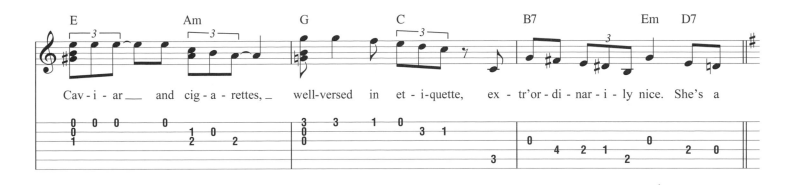

Cav-i-ar ___ and cig-a-rettes, ___ well-versed in et-i-quette, ex-tr'or-di-nar-i-ly nice. She's a

𝄋𝄋 Chorus

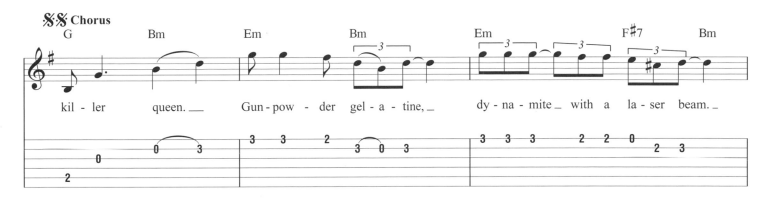

kil-ler queen. ___ Gun-pow-der gel-a-tine, ___ dy-na-mite ___ with a la-ser beam. ___

To Coda 1 ⊕

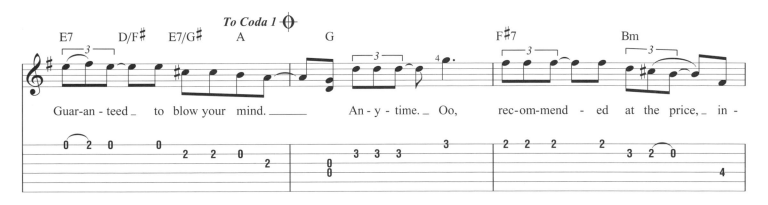

Guar-an-teed ___ to blow your mind. _____ An-y-time. ___ Oo, rec-om-mend-ed at the price, ___ in-

To Coda 2 ⊕

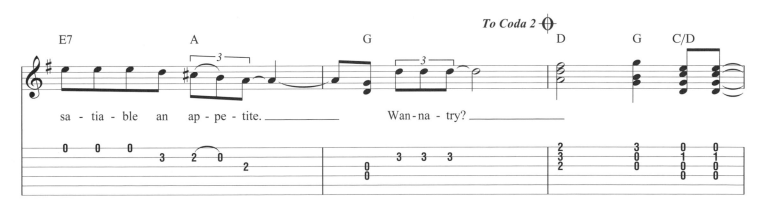

sa-tia-ble an ap-pe-tite. _____ Wan-na-try? _____

D.S. al Coda 1

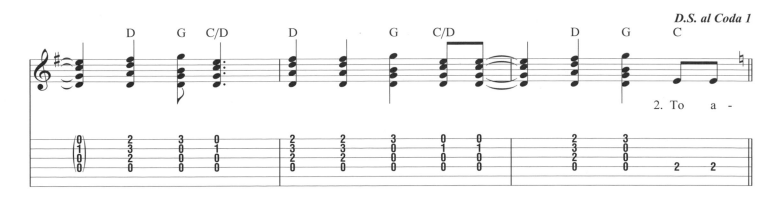

2. To a-

19

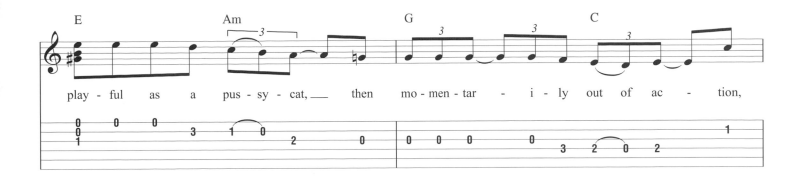

play - ful as a pus - sy - cat, ___ then mo - men - tar - i - ly out of ac - tion,

tem - po - rar - i - ly out of gas. ___ She'll ab - so - lute - ly drive you wild, ___

D.S.S. al Coda 2

⊕ **Coda 2**

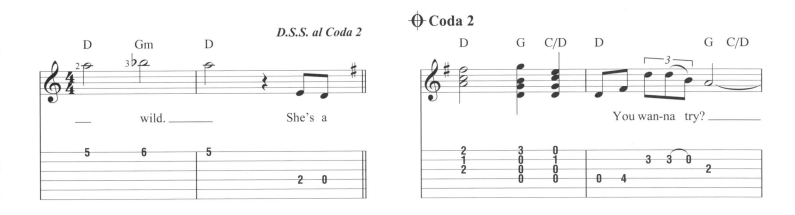

___ wild. ___ She's a   You wan-na try? ___

Outro

Repeat and fade

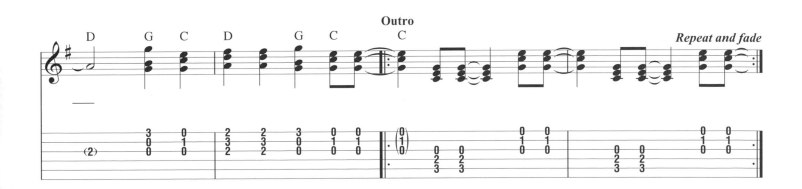

Additional Lyrics

2. To avoid complications, she never kept the same address.
In conversation, she spoke just like a baroness.
Met a man from China, went down to Geisha Minah.
Then again, incident'ly if you're that way inclined.
Perfume came naturally from Paris;
For cars, she couldn't care less, fastidious and precise.

Fat Bottomed Girls

Words and Music by Brian May

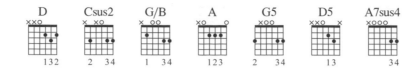

Strum Pattern: 3, 4
Pick Pattern: 1

Chorus
Moderately slow, in 2

Are _____ you gon - na take me home to - night? Ah, _____

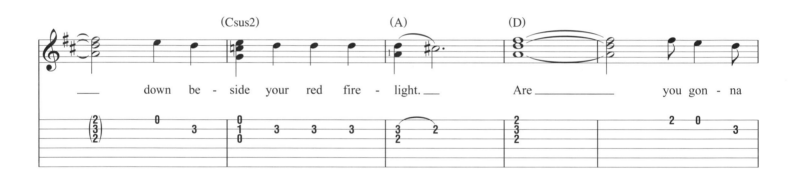

_____ down be - side your red fire - light. _____ Are _____ you gon - na

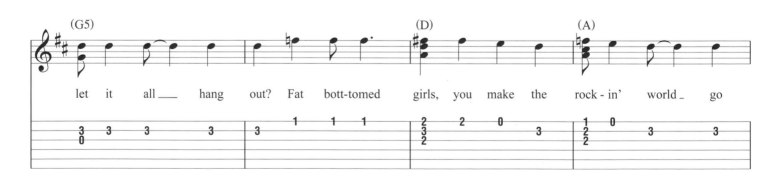

let it all ___ hang out? Fat bott-tomed girls, you make the rock-in' world ___ go

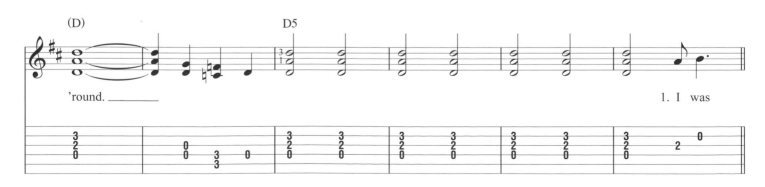

'round. _____   1. I was

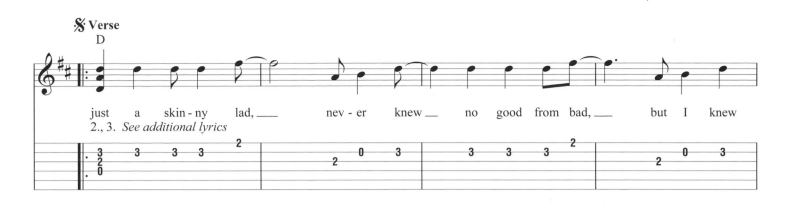

just a skin-ny lad, _____ nev-er knew _____ no good from bad, _____ but I knew
2., 3. *See additional lyrics*

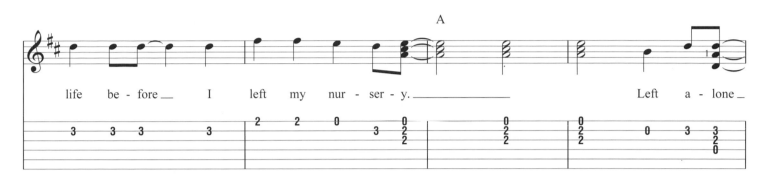

life be-fore _____ I left my nur-ser-y. _____ Left a-lone _____

_____ with big fat fan-ny, _____ she was such a naugh-ty nan-ny. Big

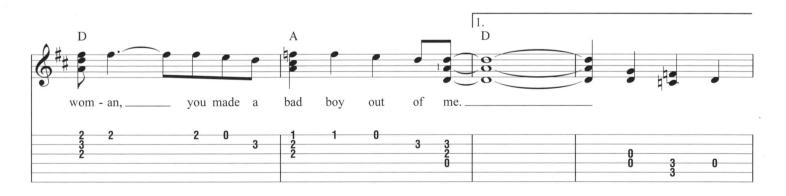

wom-an, _____ you made a bad boy out of me. _____

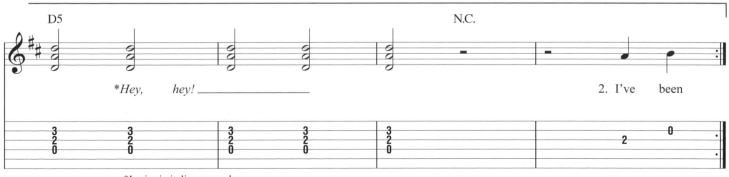

Hey, hey! _____ 2. I've been

*Lyrics in italics are spoken.

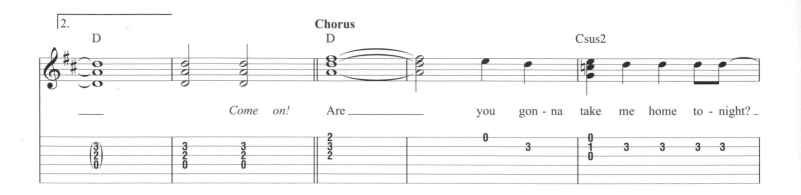

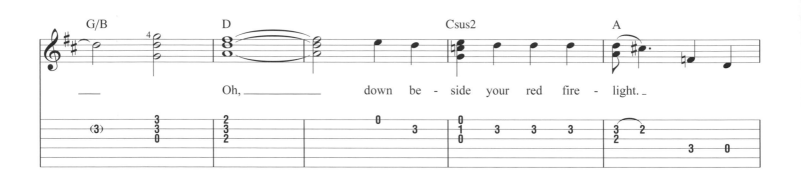

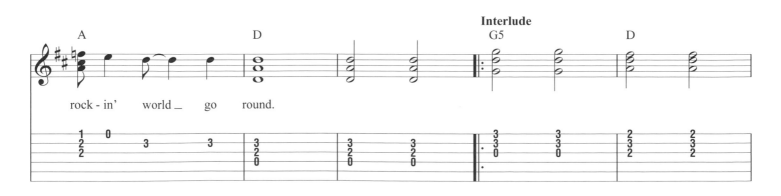

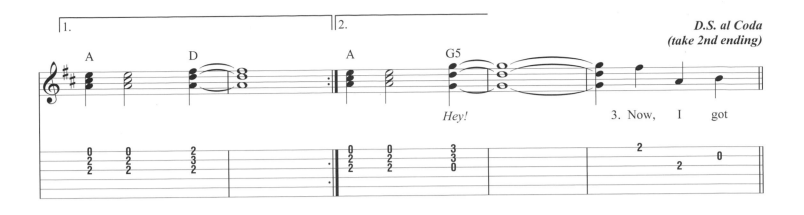

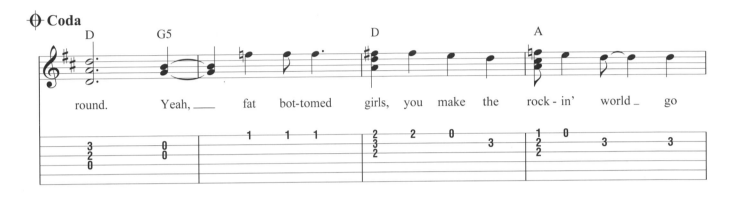

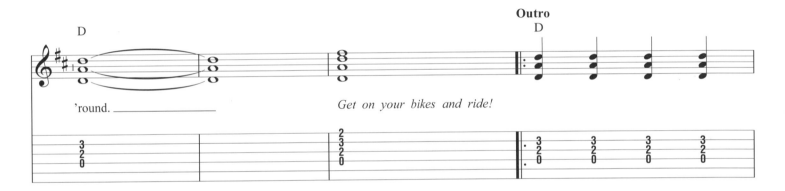

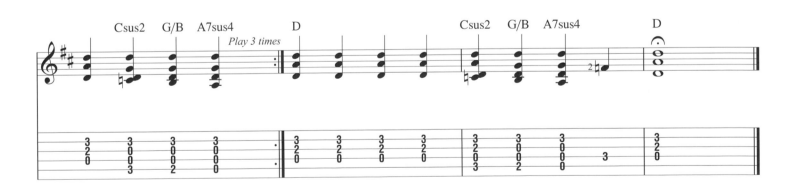

Additional Lyrics

2. I've been singin' with my band 'cross water, cross the land.
   I've seen every blue-eyed floozy on the way, hey.
   But their beauty and their style went kind of smooth after a while,
   Take me to them dirty ladies every time. *Come on!*

3. Now, I got mortgages and homes. I got stiffness in my bones.
   Ain't no beauty queens in this locality. I tell ya.
   Oh, but I still got my pleasure, still got my greatest treasure.
   Big woman, you done made a big man of me. Now hear this.

Bohemian Rhapsody

Words and Music by Freddie Mercury

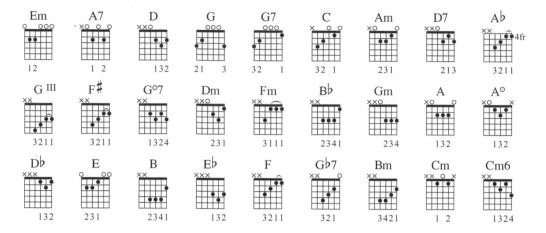

Strum Pattern: 3, 4
Pick Pattern: 2, 3

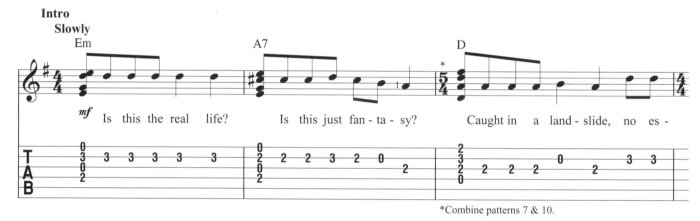

*Combine patterns 7 & 10.

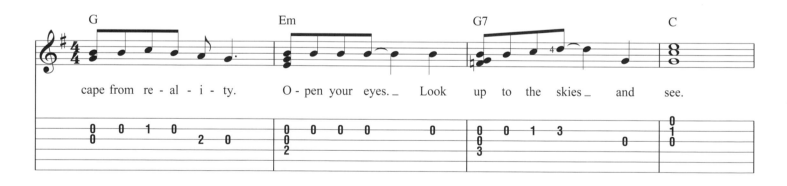

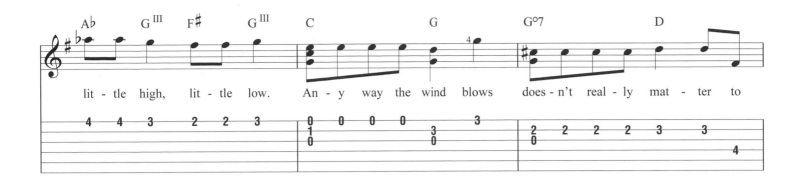

little high, little low. Any way the wind blows doesn't really matter to

me, to me. me.

Verse

1. Ma-ma, just
2. *See additional lyrics*

killed a man. Put a gun against his head, pulled my trigger, now he's dead.

Ma-ma, life had just be-gun, but now I've gone and thrown it all a-way.

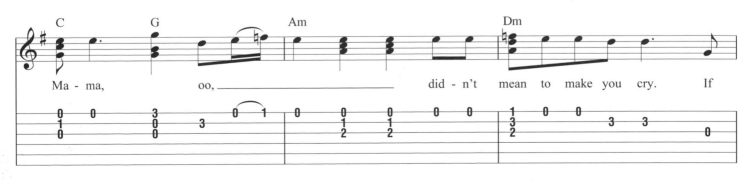

Ma-ma, oo, didn't mean to make you cry. If

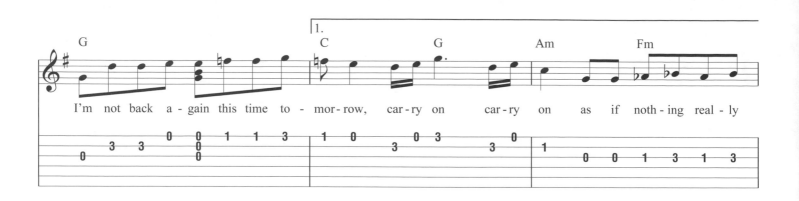

I'm not back a-gain this time to-mor-row, car-ry on car-ry on as if noth-ing real-ly

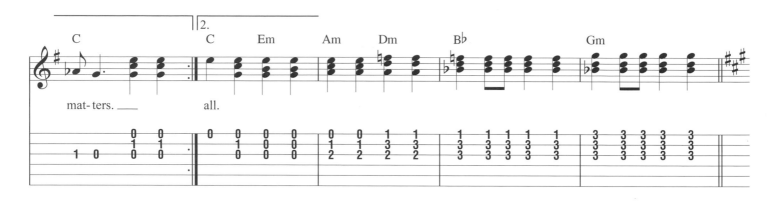

mat-ters. ___ all.

Interlude
Faster

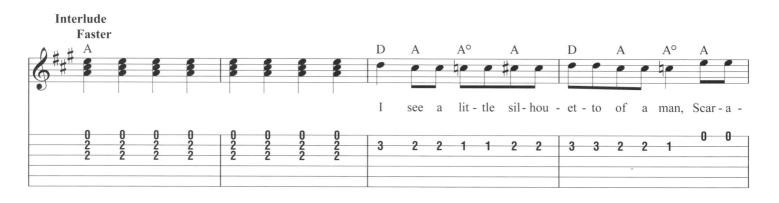

I see a lit-tle sil-hou-et-to of a man, Scar-a-

mouche, Scar-a-mouche, will you do the Fan-dan-go. Thun-der bolt and light-ning, ver-y, ver-y fright-'ning

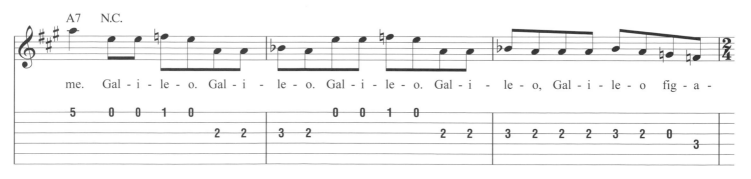

me. Gal-i-le-o. Gal-i-le-o. Gal-i-le-o. Gal-i-le-o, Gal-i-le-o fig-a-

ro Mag - ni - fi - co. _____ I'm just a poor boy and no - bod - y loves me.

*Use Pattern 10

He's just a poor boy from a poor fam - i - ly. Spare him his life from this mon - stros - i - ty.

Eas - y come, eas - y go, will you let me go? Bis - mil - lah! No, we

will not let you go. Let him go! _____ Bis - mil - lah! We will not let you go. Let him go! _

_____ Bis - mil - lah! We will not let you go. Let me go. Will not let you go. Let me go.

Will not let you go. Let me go. Ah. _____ No, no, no, no, no, no, no. Oh ma-ma

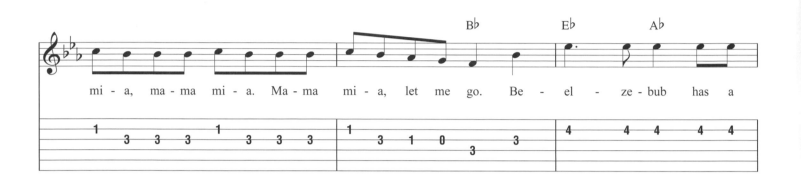

mi-a, ma-ma mi-a. Ma-ma mi-a, let me go. Be-el-ze-bub has a

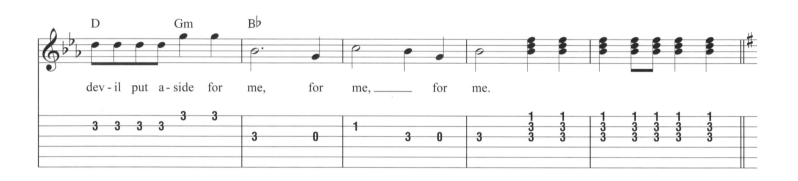

dev-il put a-side for me, for me, _____ for me.

Chorus

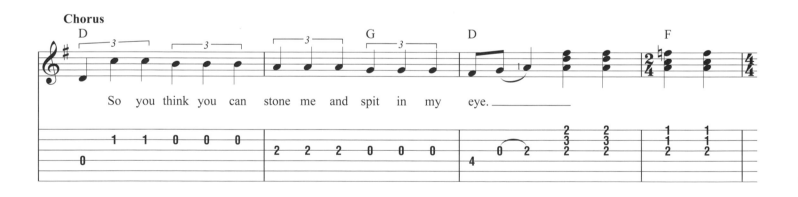

So you think you can stone me and spit in my eye. _____

So you think you can love me and leave me to die. _____ Oh, _____

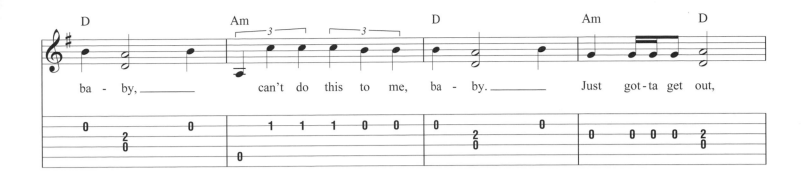

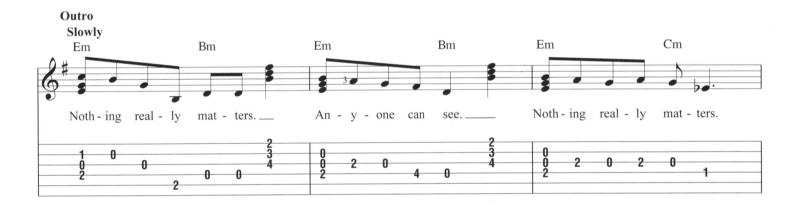

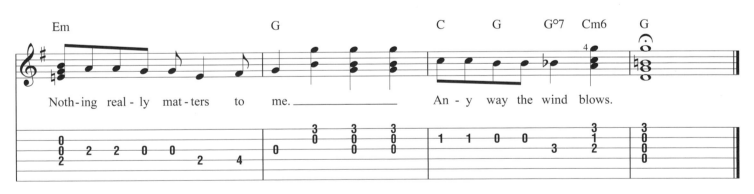

Additional Lyrics

2. Too late, my time has come.
   Sends shivers down my spine, body's aching all the time.
   Goodbye ev'ry body, I've got to go.
   Gotta leave you all behind and face the truth.
   Mama, oo, I don't want to die.
   I sometimes wish I'd never been born at all.

Now I'm Here

Words and Music by Brian May

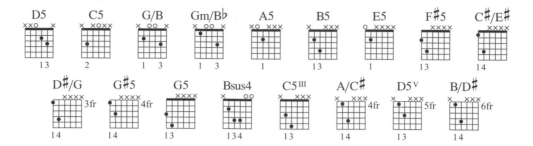

Strum Pattern: 1, 2
Pick Pattern: 2, 4

Intro
Moderately fast

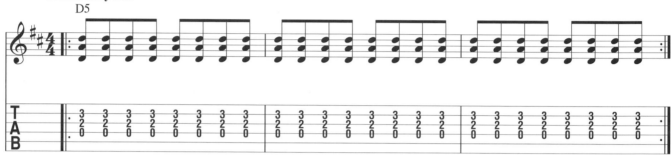

Verse

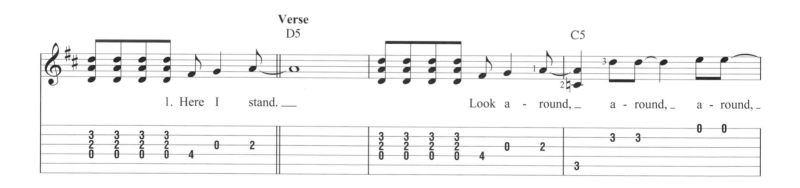

1. Here I stand. ___ Look a - round, ___ a - round, ___ a - round, ___

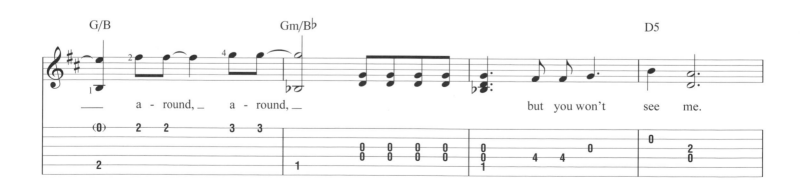

___ a - round, ___ a - round, ___ but you won't see me.

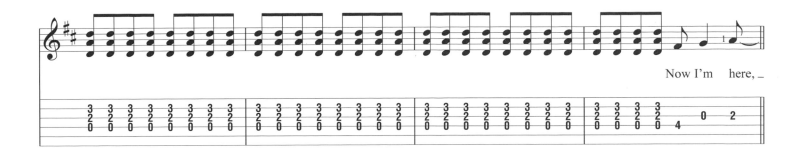

Now I'm here, —

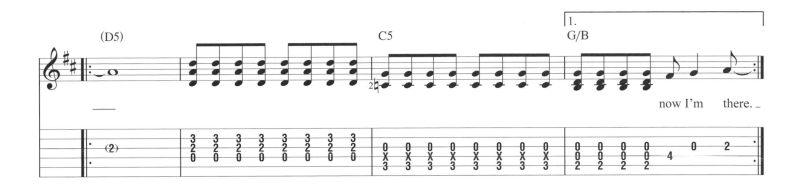

now I'm there. —

*I'm just...

*Lyrics in italics are spoken.

Just a new — man. — Yes, you made — me live a - gain. —

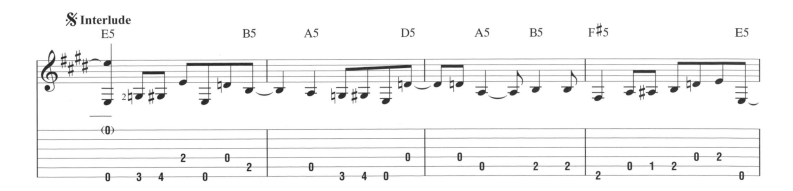

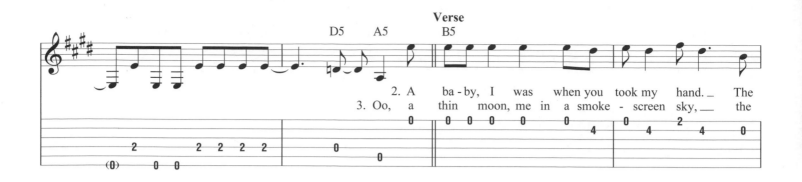

Verse

2. A ba-by, I was when you took my hand. _ The
3. Oo, a thin moon, me in a smoke-screen sky, _ the

light of the night _ burned bright. _ The peo-ple all stared, did-n't
beams of your love - light chase. _ Don't move, _____ don't speak, don't _

To Coda ⊕

un-der-stand, _____ but you knew my name on sight. _____ Oo, what-
feel no pain. _____ The rain run-in' down my face. _

Chorus

ev - er came _ of you _ and me, _ A - mer - i - ca's _ new bride _ to be. _

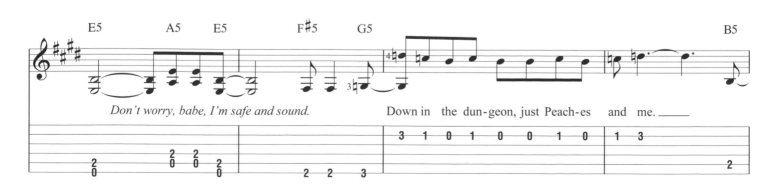

Don't worry, babe, I'm safe and sound. Down in the dun-geon, just Peach-es and me. ___

34

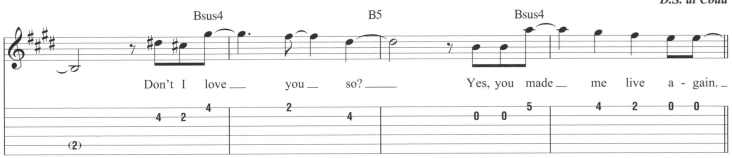

Don't I love ___ you ___ so? ___ Yes, you made ___ me live a-gain. ___

⊕ **Coda**

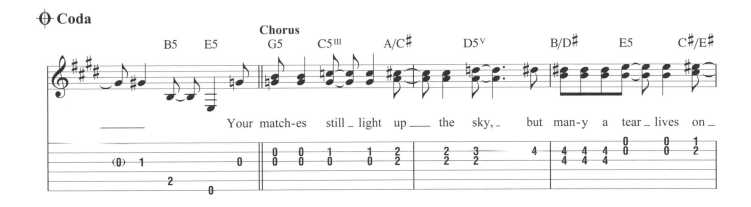

___ Your match-es still ___ light up ___ the sky, ___ but man-y a tear ___ lives on ___

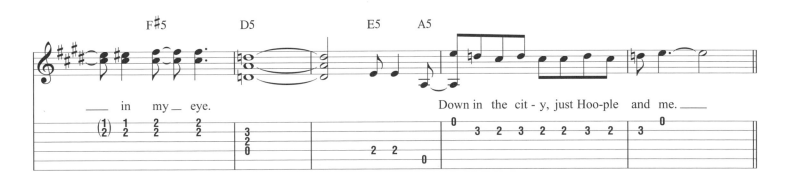

___ in my ___ eye. Down in the cit-y, just Hoo-ple and me. ___

Interlude

What-

Chorus

ev-er comes ___ of you ___ and me, ___ I'd love to leave ___ my mem ___ o-ry ___ with you. ___

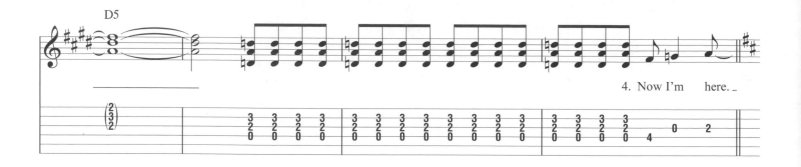

Verse

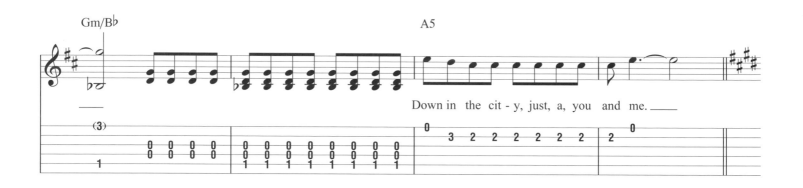

Think I'll stay ___ a - round, ___ a - round, ___ a - round, ___ a - round.

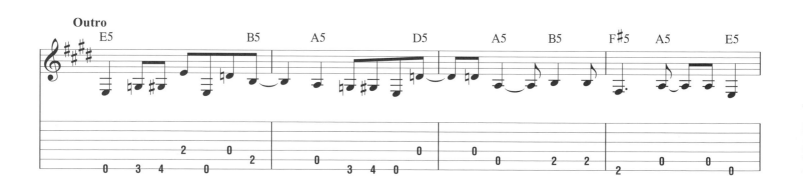

Down in the cit - y, just, a, you and me. ___

Outro

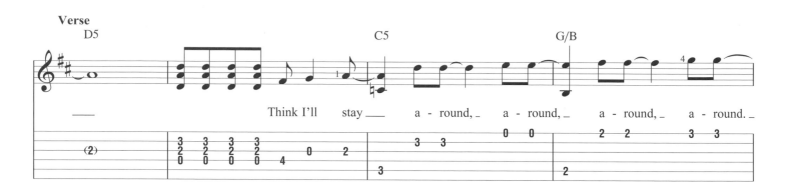

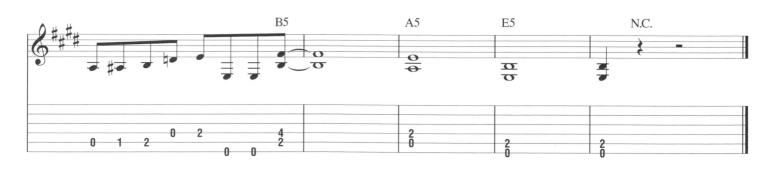

Love of My Life

Words and Music by Freddie Mercury

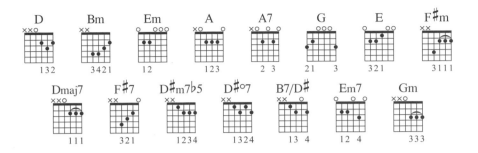

Strum Pattern: 3, 4
Pick Pattern: 3, 4

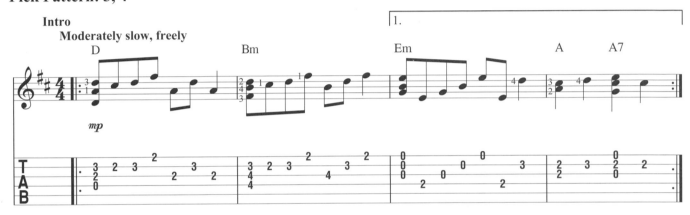

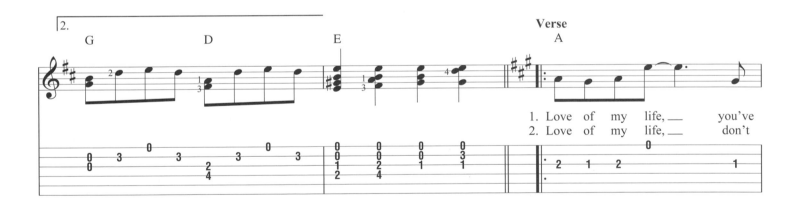

1. Love of my life, ___ you've
2. Love of my life, ___ don't

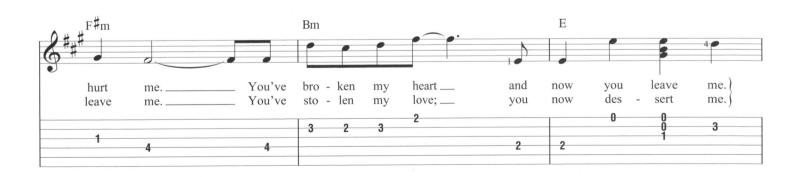

hurt me. ___ You've bro-ken my heart ___ and now you leave me.
leave me. ___ You've sto-len my love; ___ you now des-ert me.

Crazy Little Thing Called Love

Words and Music by Freddie Mercury

Strum Pattern: 1
Pick Pattern: 3

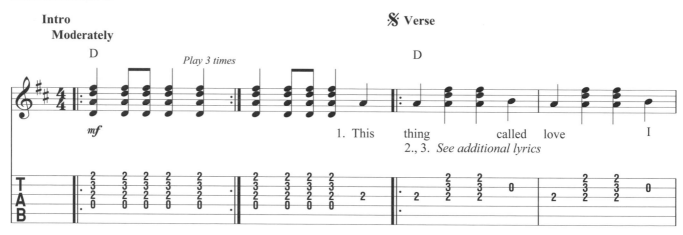

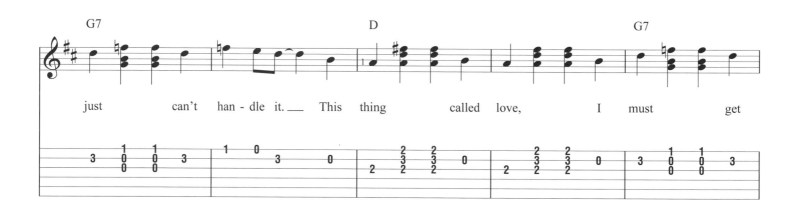

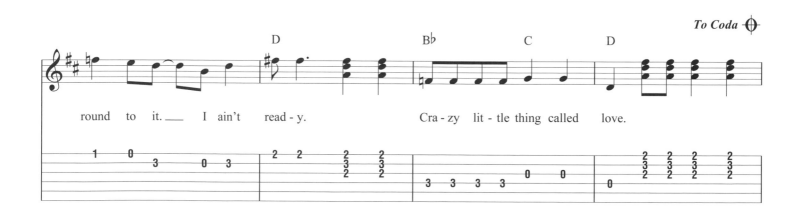

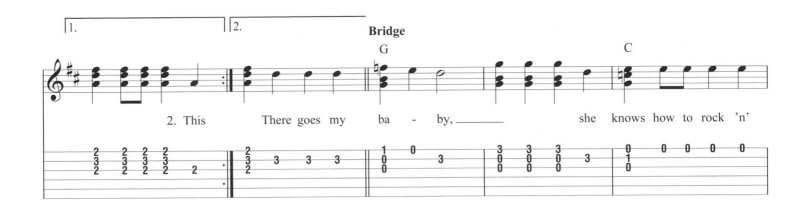

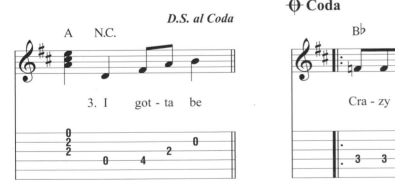

D.S. al Coda

⊕ **Coda**

Repeat and fade

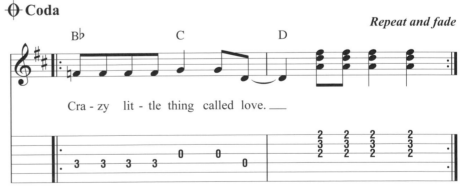

Additional Lyrics

2. This thing called love,
   It cries (like a baby) in a cradle all night.
   It swings, it jives,
   It shakes all over like a jellyfish.
   I kinda' like it.
   Crazy little thing called love.

3. I gotta be cool, relax,
   Get hip, get on my tracks.
   Take a backseat, hitchhike,
   And take a long ride on my motor bike
   Until I'm ready.
   Crazy little thing called love.

We Will Rock You

Words and Music by Brian May

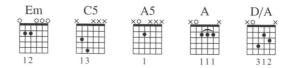

Strum Pattern: 1
Pick Pattern: 1

Verse
Moderately, in 2

1. Bud - dy, you're a boy, make a big noise play - in' in the street, gon - na be a big
2., 3. *See additional lyrics*

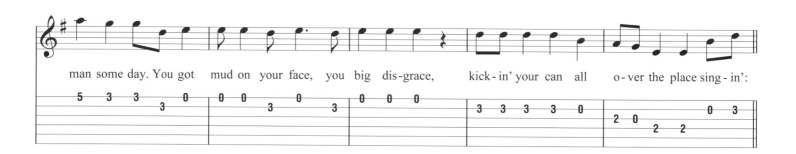

man some day. You got mud on your face, you big dis-grace, kick-in' your can all o-ver the place sing-in':

Chorus

1., 2.

We will, we will rock you. We will, we will rock you.

3.

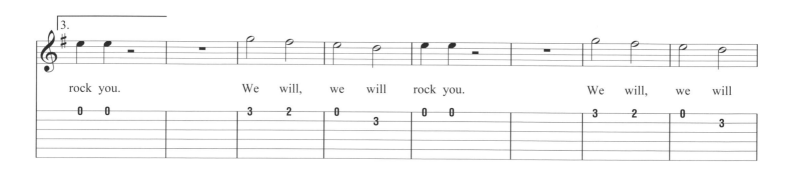

rock you. We will, we will rock you. We will, we will

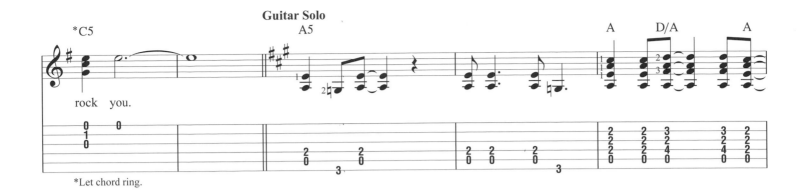

*Let chord ring.

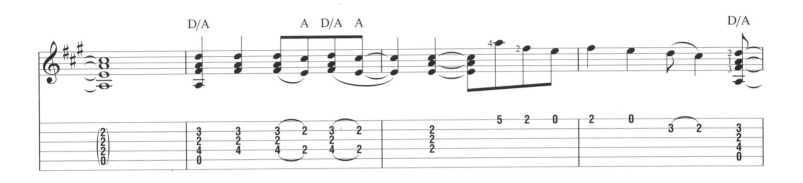

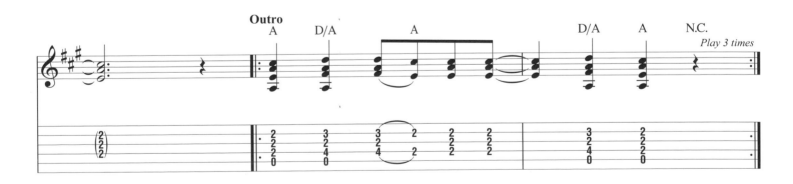

Additional Lyrics

2. Buddy, you're a young man, hard man shoutin' in the street,
   Gonna take on the world some day.
   You got blood on your face,
   You big disgrace,
   Wavin' your banner all over the place.

3. Buddy, you're an old man, poor man pleadin' with your eyes,
   Gonna make you some peace someday.
   You got mud on your face,
   You big disgrace,
   Somebody better put you back into your place.

Another One Bites the Dust

Words and Music by John Deacon

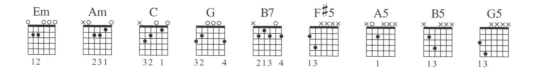

*Tune down 1/2 step:
(low to high) Eb-Ab-Db-Gb-Bb-Eb

Strum Pattern: 1, 4
Pick Pattern: 3, 5

Intro
Moderately
N.C.

mf

*Optional: To match recording, tune down 1/2 step.

Play 4 times

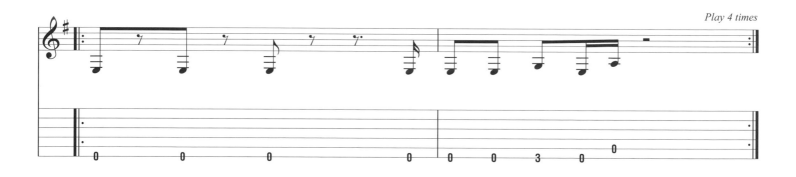

℗ Verse
**Em
***

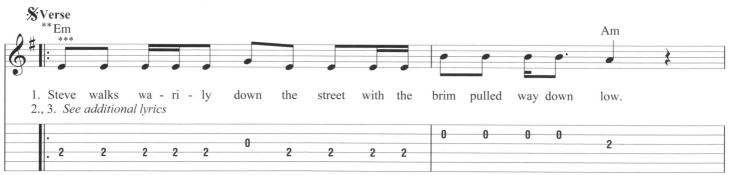

1. Steve walks wa-ri-ly down the street with the brim pulled way down low.
2., 3. *See additional lyrics*

**Chords are implied.
*** 2nd & 3rd time, sung one octave higher.

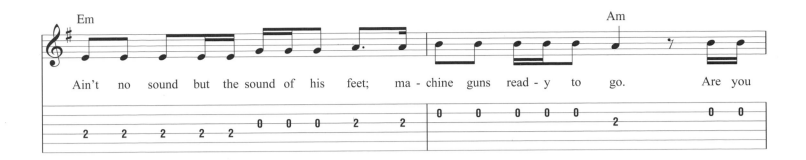

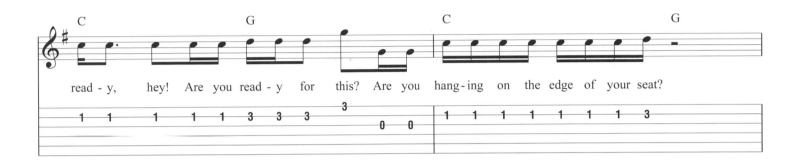

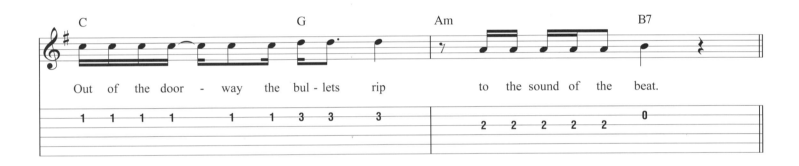

Chorus

oth - er one gone and an - oth - er one gone. An - oth - er one bites the dust.

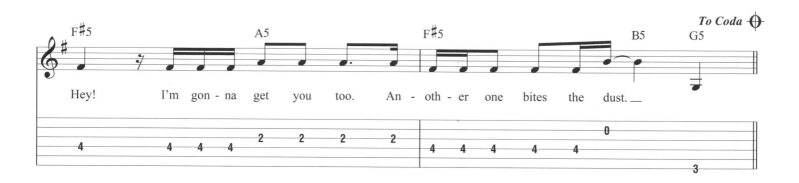

Hey! I'm gon - na get you too. An - oth - er one bites the dust. __

1.
Interlude
N.C.

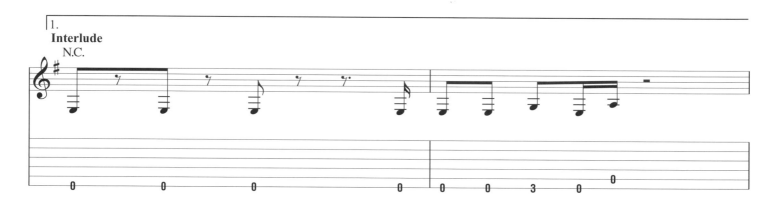

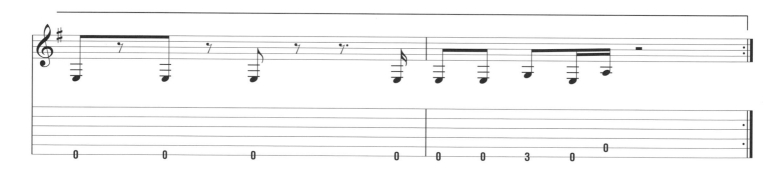

2.
Breakdown
N.C.

An -

oth - er one bites the dust. An - oth - er one bites the dust. Hey, _____

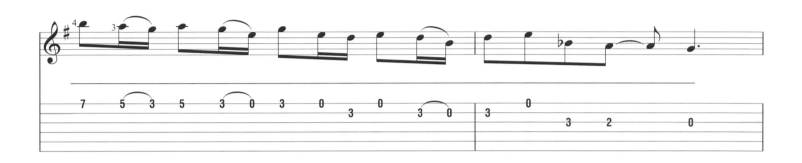

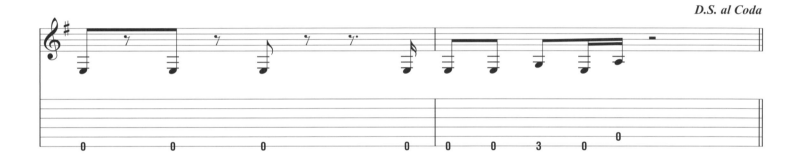

⊕ Coda

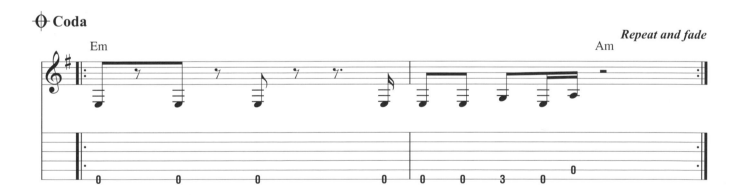

Additional Lyrics

2. How do you think I'm going to get along
   Without you, when you're gone?
   You took me for ev'rything that I had
   And kicked me out on my own.
   Are you happy? Are you satisfied?
   How long can you stand the heat?
   Out of the doorway the bullets rip
   To the sound of the beat.

3. There are plenty of ways you can hurt a man,
   And bring him to the ground.
   You can beat him, you can cheat him,
   You can treat him bad and leave him when he's down.
   But I'm ready, yes I'm ready for you.
   I'm standing on my own two feet.
   Out of the doorway the bullets rip,
   Repeating the sound of the beat.

I Want to Break Free

Words and Music by John Deacon

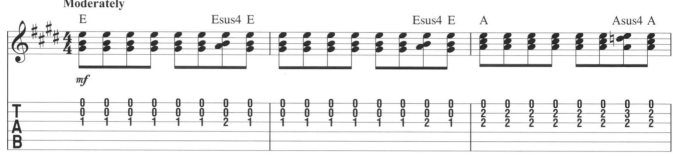

Strum Pattern: 1
Pick Pattern: 5

Moderately

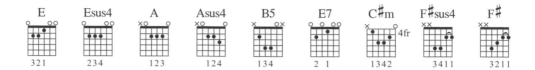

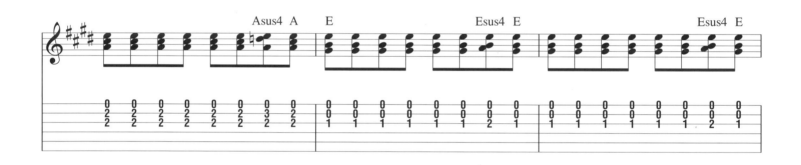

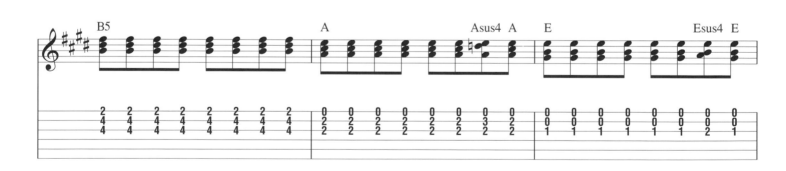

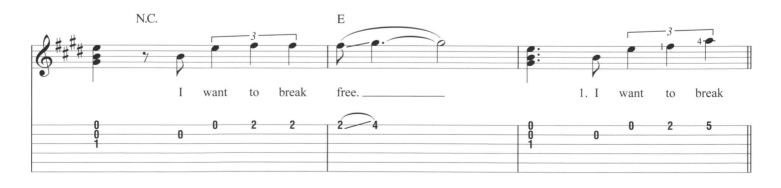

I want to break free. _____

1. I want to break

walk out that door. _____ Oh, how I want to be free, ba-by. Oh, how I want to be

D.S al Coda

free. _____ Oh, how I want to break _____ free. _____ 3. But life still goes

Coda

own. _____ So, ba-by, can't you see _____ I've got to break free. _____

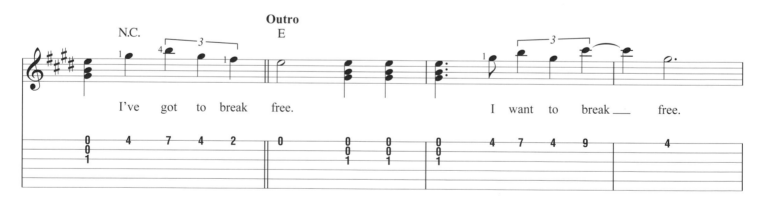

Outro

I've got to break free. I want to break _____ free.

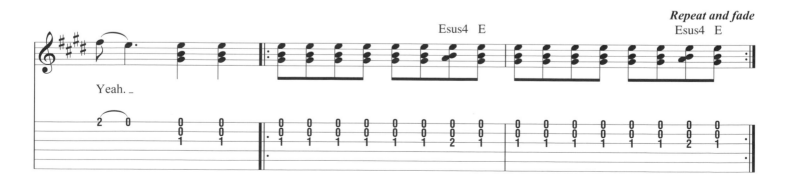

Repeat and fade

Yeah. _

Under Pressure

Words and Music by Freddie Mercury, John Deacon, Brian May, Roger Taylor and David Bowie

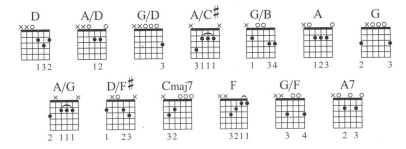

Strum Pattern: 1, 4
Pick Pattern: 2, 4

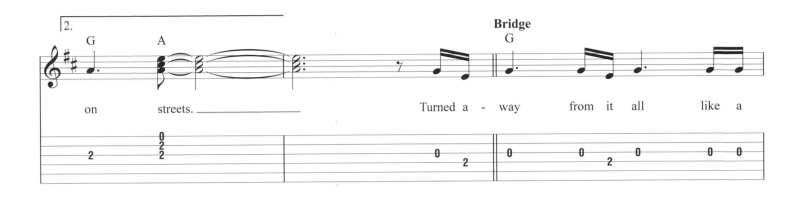

on streets._____ Turned a - way from it all like a

blind man; sat on a fence, __ but it don't work._____ Keep

com - ing up with love, but it's so slashed and torn. __ Why?_____ Why?_____

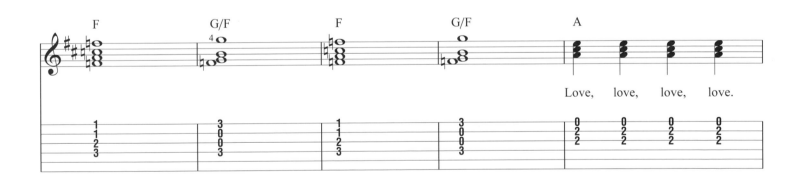

Love, love, love, love.

In - san - i - ty laughs, _ un - der pres - sure we're crack - ing. Can't we

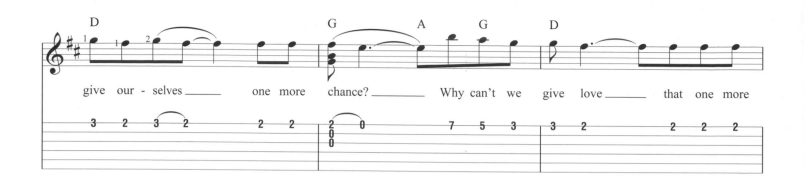

give our-selves _____ one more chance? _____ Why can't we give love _____ that one more

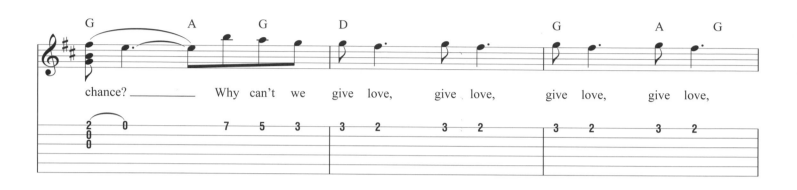

chance? _____ Why can't we give love, give love, give love, give love,

give love, give love, give love, give love? 'Cause love's such _ an old-fash - ioned

word, and _ love dares you _ to care for _ the peo - ple on the

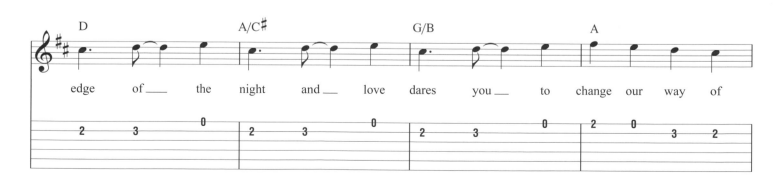

edge of _ the night and _ love dares you _ to change our way of

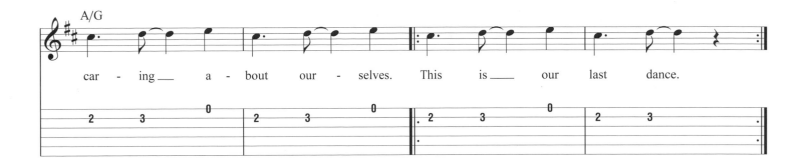

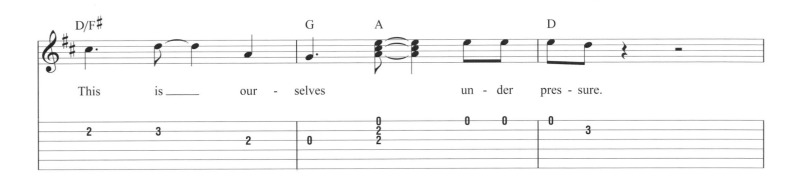

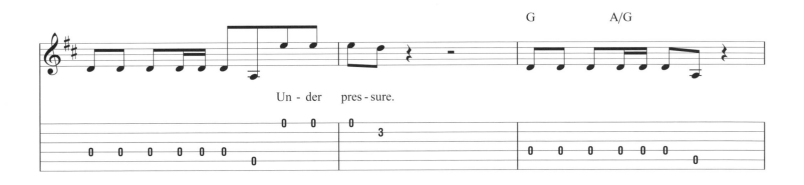

Additional Lyrics

2. Chippin' around, kick my brains around the floor.
These are the days it never rains but it pours.
People on streets.
People on streets.

Who Wants to Live Forever

Words and Music by Brian May

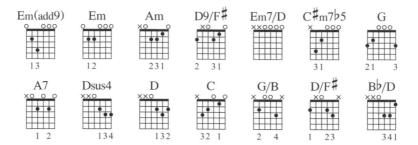

Strum Pattern: 6
Pick Pattern: 2

Intro
Slow, freely

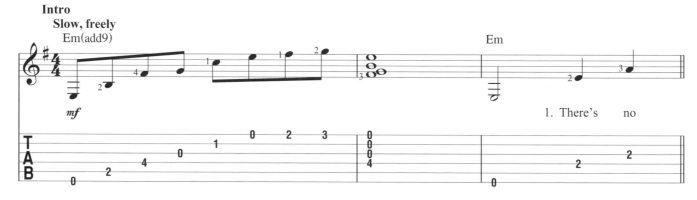

1. There's no

Verse

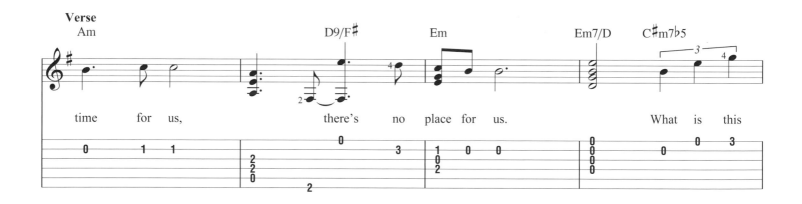

time for us, there's no place for us. What is this

thing that builds our dreams yet slips a-way from us? _____ Who

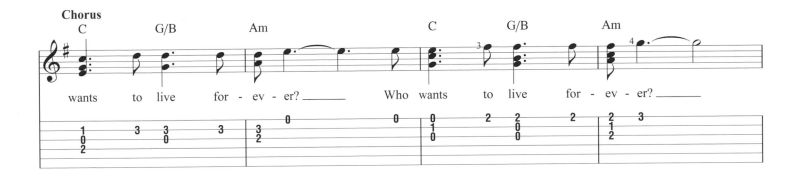

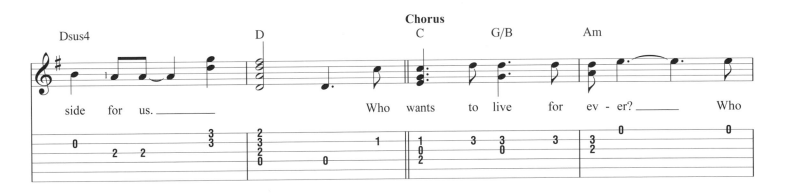

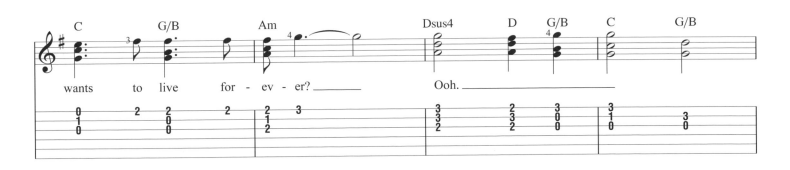

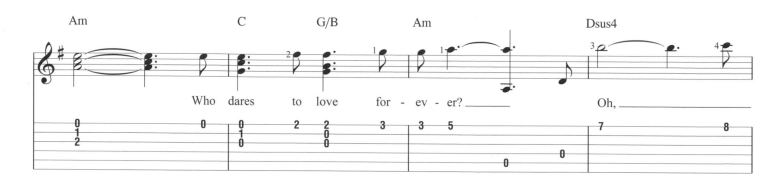

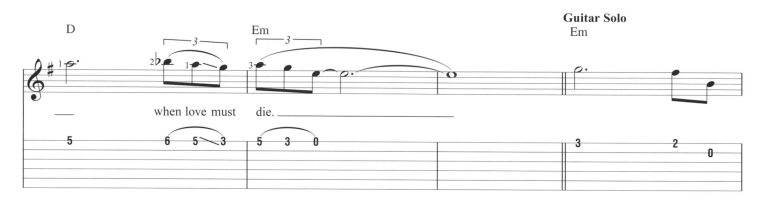

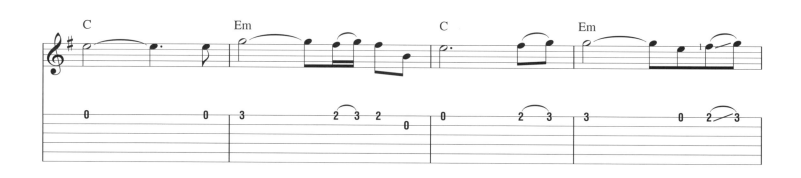

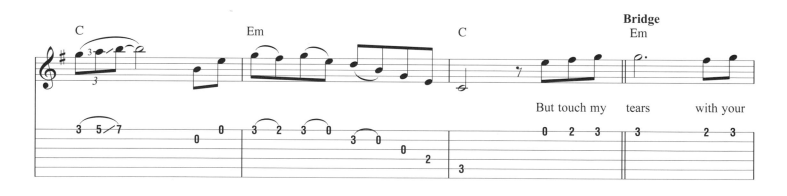

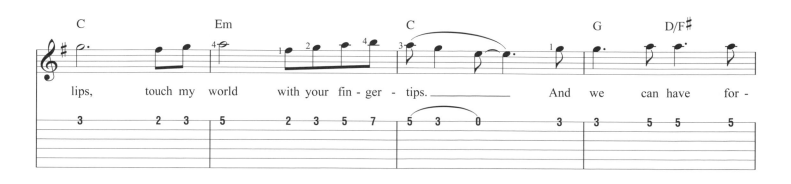

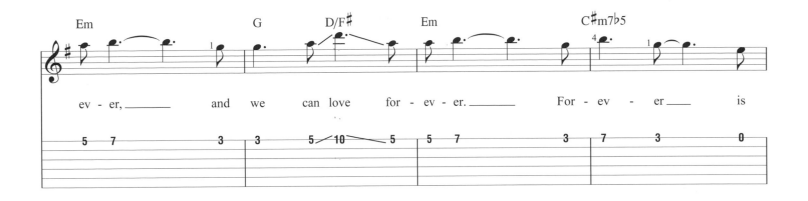

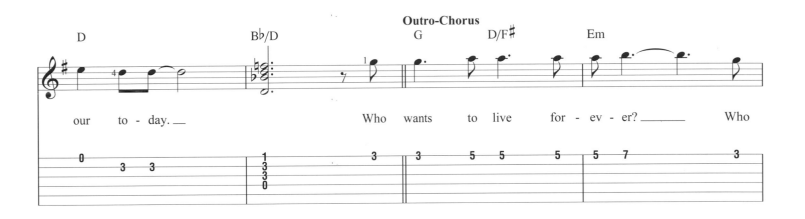

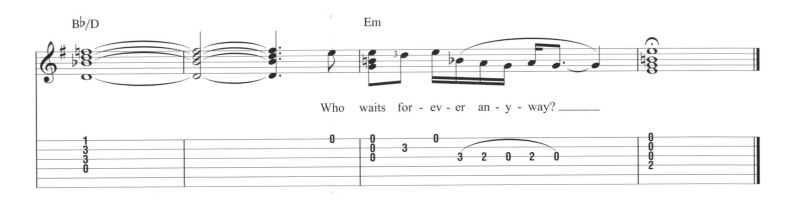

Radio Ga Ga

Words and Music by Roger Taylor

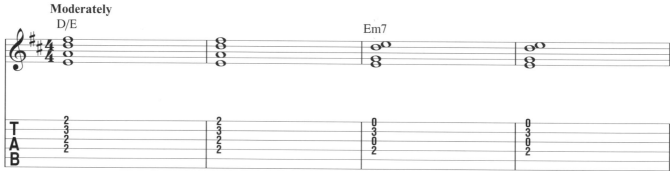

*Capo III

Strum Pattern: 5
Pick Pattern: 2

Intro
Moderately

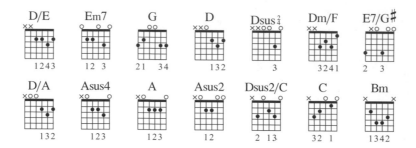

*Optional: To match recording, place capo at 3rd fret.

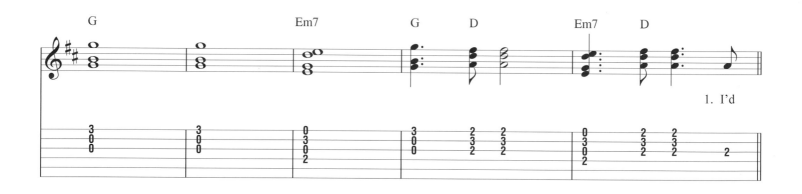

1. I'd

sit a - lone ___ and watch your light, ___ my on - ly friend _ through

2., 3. *See additional lyrics*

teen - age nights. _ And ev - 'ry - thing _ I had to know, _ I

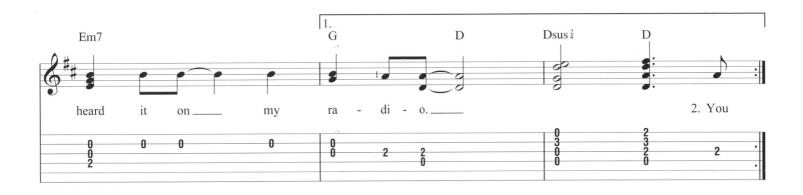

heard it on _ my ra - di - o. _

2. You

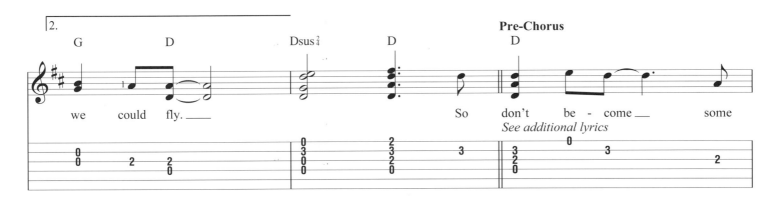

we could fly. _

Pre-Chorus

So don't be - come _ some

See additional lyrics

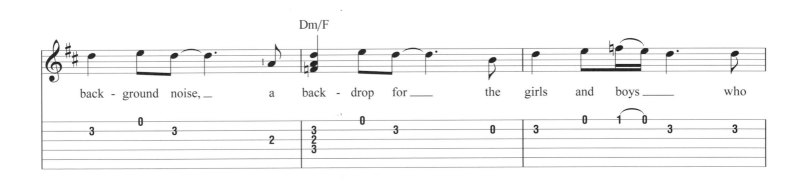

back - ground noise, _ a back - drop for _ the girls and boys _ who

just don't know _ or just don't care, _ and just com - plain _ when

you're not there. ___ You had your time; ___ you had your pow'r. ___ You've

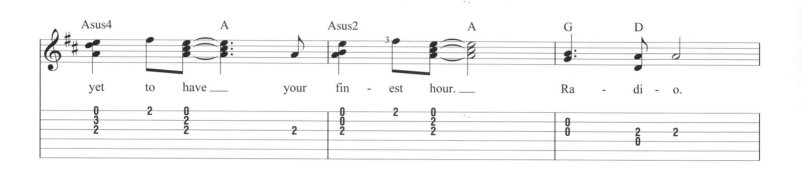

yet to have ___ your fin - est hour. ___ Ra - di - o.

Chorus

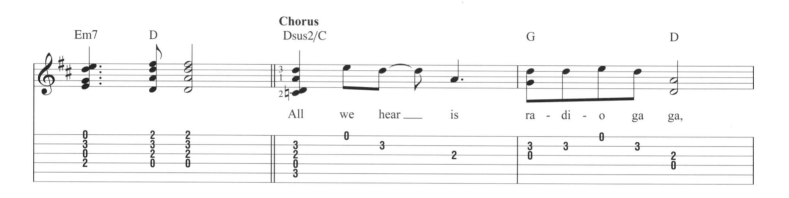

All we hear ___ is ra - di - o ga ga,

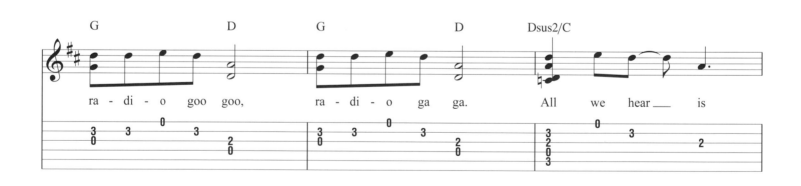

ra - di - o goo goo, ra - di - o ga ga. All we hear ___ is

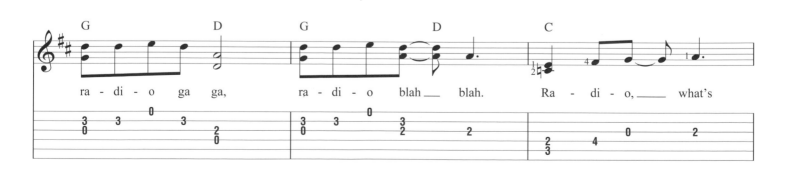

ra - di - o ga ga, ra - di - o blah ___ blah. Ra - di - o, ___ what's

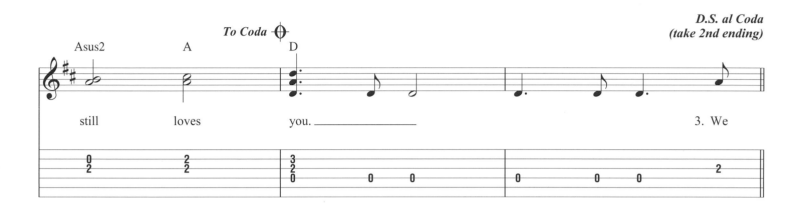

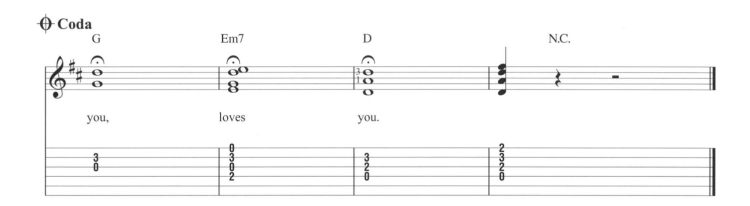

Additional Lyrics

2. You gave them all those old-time stars,
   Through wars of worlds, invaded by Mars.
   You made 'em laugh; you made 'em cry.
   You made us feel like we could fly.

3. We watch the shows; we watch the stars
   On videos for hours and hours.
   We hardly need to use our ears.
   How music changes through the years.

Pre-Chorus: Let's hope you never leave, old friend.
   Like all good things, on you we depend.
   So stick around, 'cause we might miss you
   When we grow tired of all this visual.
   You had your time; you had your pow'r.
   You've yet to have your finest hour.
   Radio.

Hammer to Fall

Words and Music by Brian May

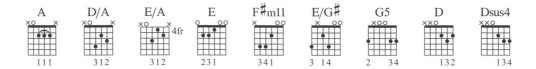

Strum Pattern: 6, 2
Pick Pattern: 3

Intro
Moderately fast

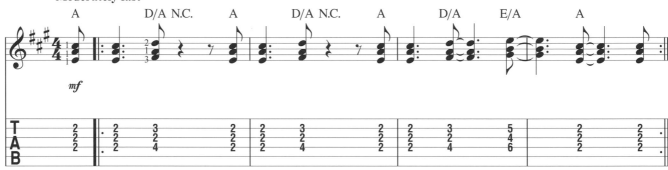

%· Verse

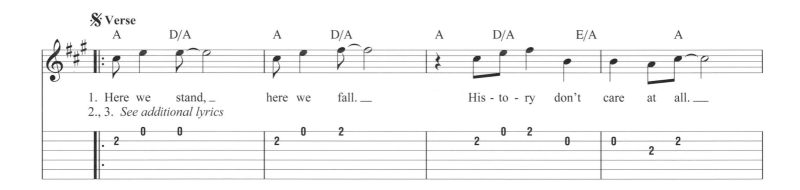

1. Here we stand, here we fall. His-to-ry don't care at all.
2., 3. *See additional lyrics*

Make the bed, light the light. La-dy Mer-cy won't be home to-night.

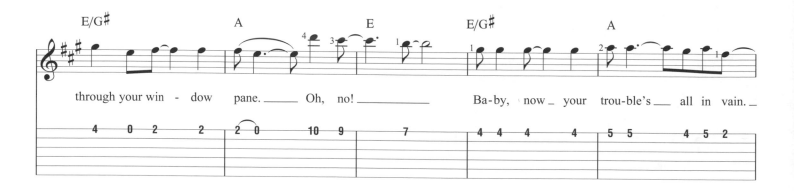

through your win - dow pane.___ Oh, no!___ Ba-by, now_ your trou-ble's_ all in vain.___

Guitar Solo

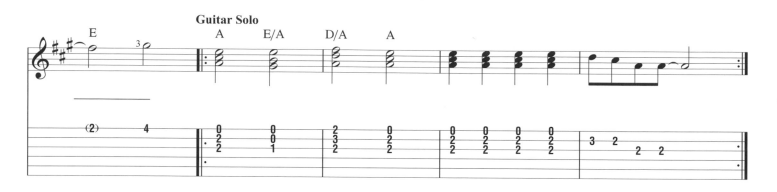

D.S. al Coda

3. For

⊕ Coda

Outro

then it's time for the ham - mer to, ham - mer to fall.

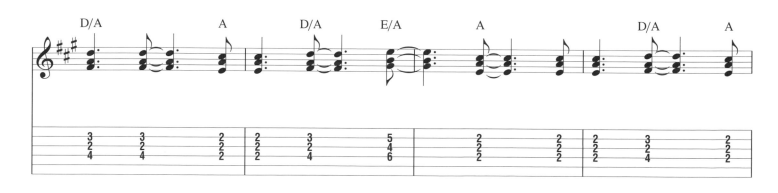

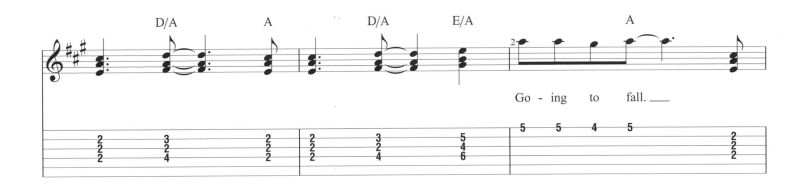

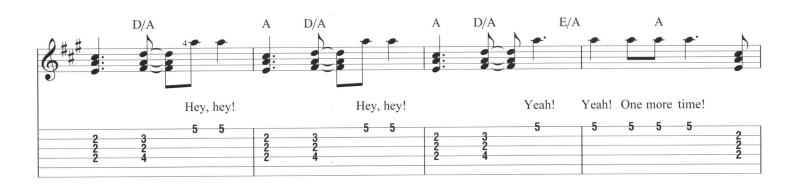

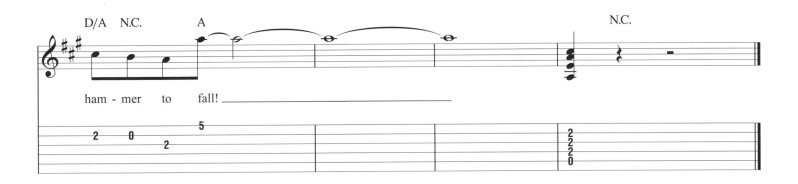

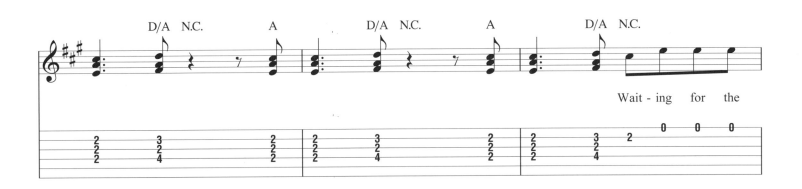

Additional Lyrics

2. Every night and every day,
   A little piece of you is fallin' away.
   Lift your face the Western way,
   Build your muscles as your body decays.

Chorus 2: Toe your line and play their game
   'Til the anaesthetic covers it all.
   'Til one day they call your name, yeah.
   Then it's time for the hammer to fall.

3. For you who grew up tall and proud,
   In the shadow of the mushroom cloud.
   Convinced our voices can't be heard,
   Just wanna scream it louder and louder and louder.

Chorus 3: What the hell we fightin' for?
   Just surrender and it won't hurt at all.
   Just got time to say your prayers,
   Then it's time for the hammer to, hammer to fall.

Don't Stop Me Now

Words and Music by Freddie Mercury

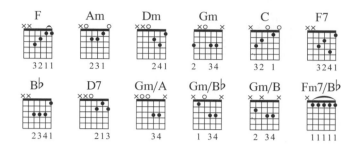

Strum Pattern: 3, 4
Pick Pattern: 4, 5

Intro
Moderately slow

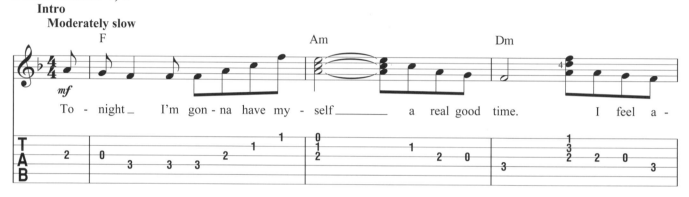

To - night __ I'm gon - na have my - self __ a real good time. I feel a -

live, _____ and the world turn - ing in - side

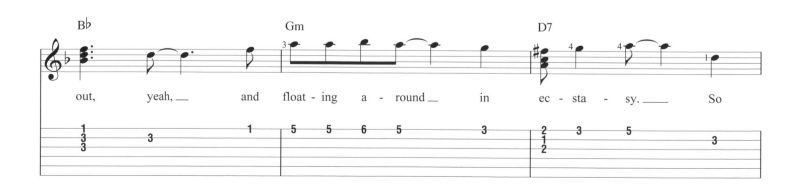

out, yeah, __ and float - ing a - round __ in ec - sta - sy. __ So

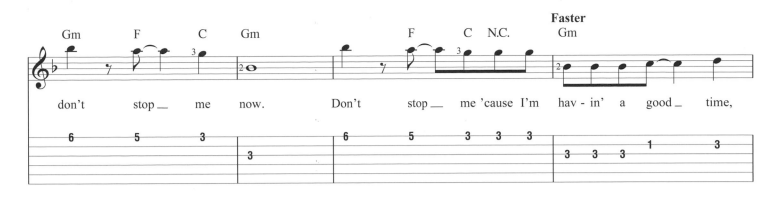

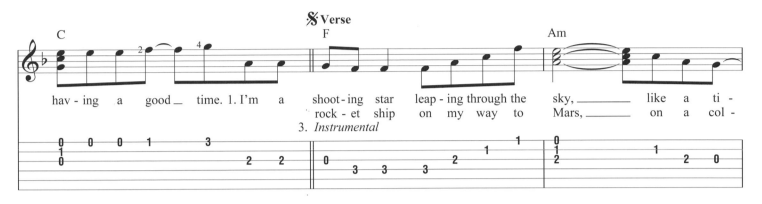

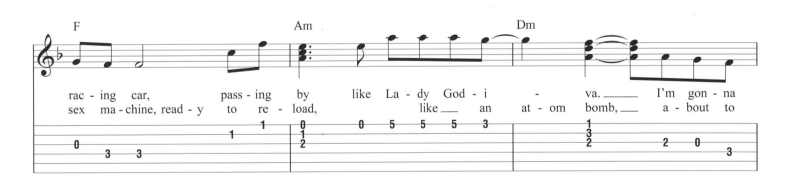

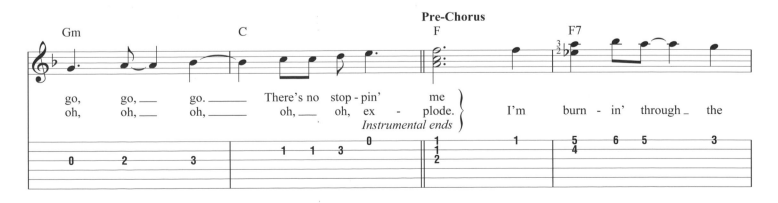

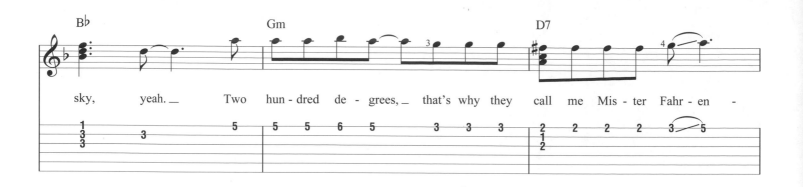

sky, yeah.__ Two hun-dred de-grees,__ that's why they call me Mis-ter Fahr-en -

heit. I'm trav-'ling at the speed of light.____ I wan-na make a

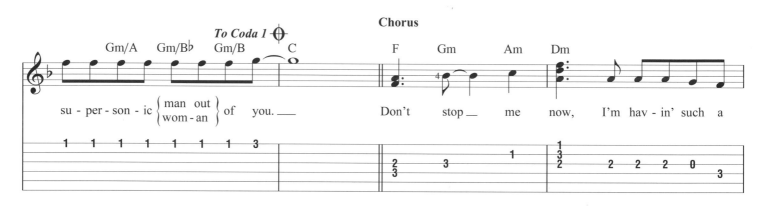

su-per-son-ic { man out / wom-an } of you.__ Don't stop__ me now, I'm hav-in' such a

good time, I'm hav-in' a ball.__ Don't stop__ me now, if you wan-na have a

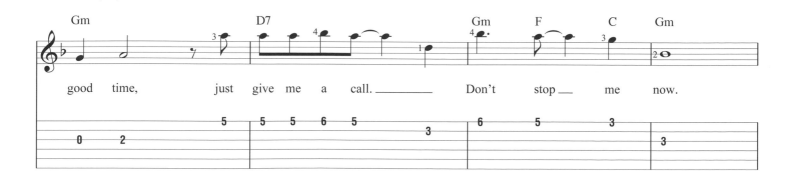

good time, just give me a call._____ Don't stop__ me now.

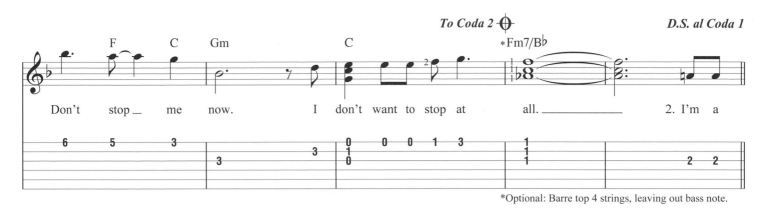

*Optional: Barre top 4 strings, leaving out bass note.

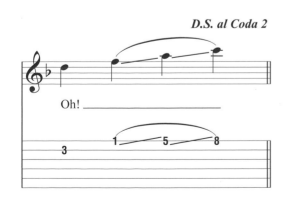

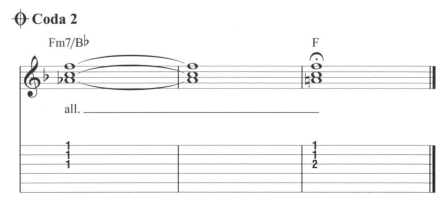

The Show Must Go On

Words and Music by Freddie Mercury, Brian May, Roger Taylor and John Deacon

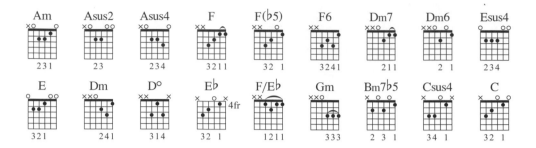

Strum Pattern: 1, 4
Pick Pattern: 2, 5

Intro
Moderately slow

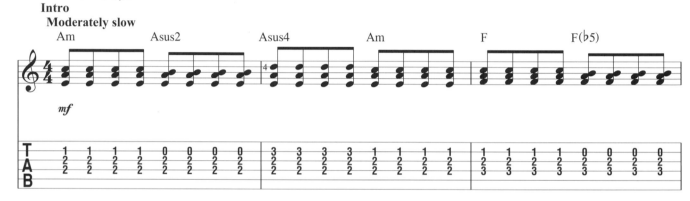

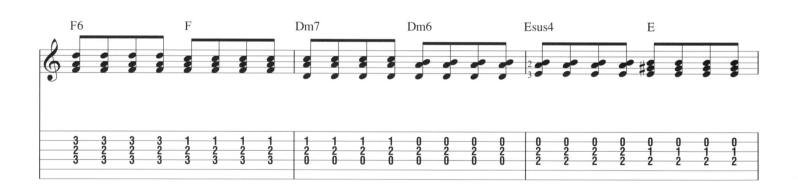

Verse

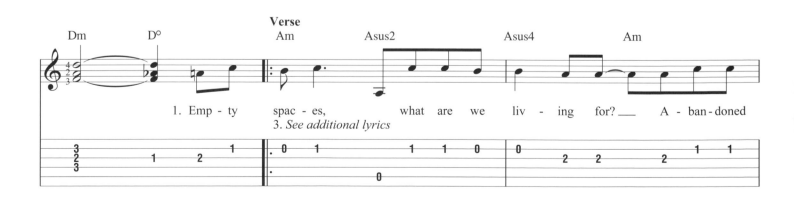

1. Emp-ty spac-es, what are we liv-ing for?___ A-ban-doned
3. *See additional lyrics*

Additional Lyrics

3. Whatever happens, I'll leave it all to chance.
Another heartache, another failed romance.
On and on, does anybody know what we are living for?

4. I guess I'm learning; I must be warmer now.
I'll soon be turning 'round the corner now.
Outside the dawn is breaking, but inside in the dark I'm aching to be free.

We Are the Champions

Words and Music by Freddie Mercury

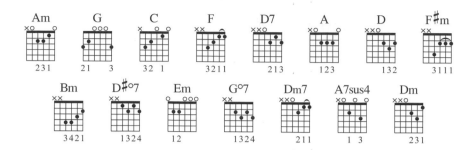

Strum Pattern: 8
Pick Pattern: 8

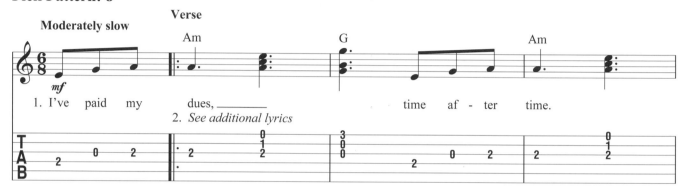

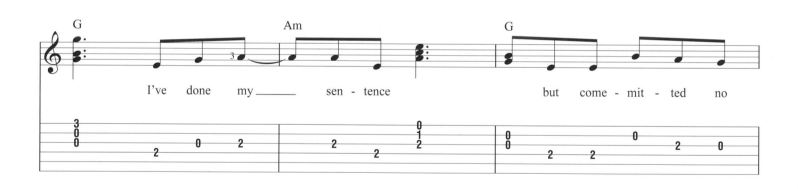

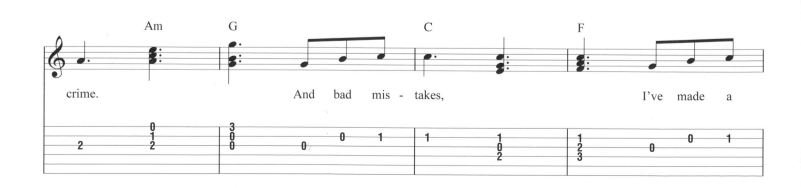

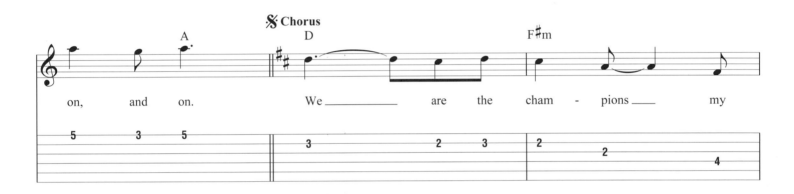

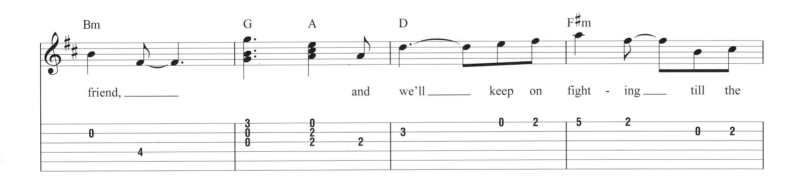

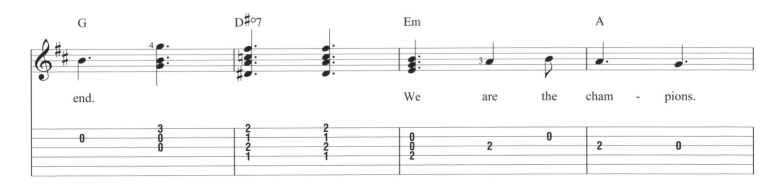

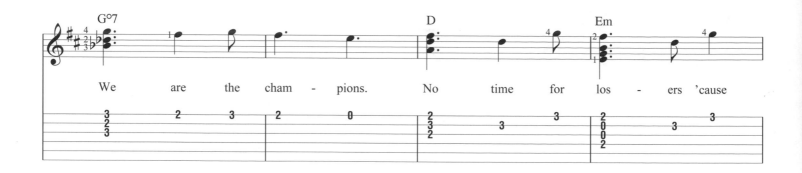

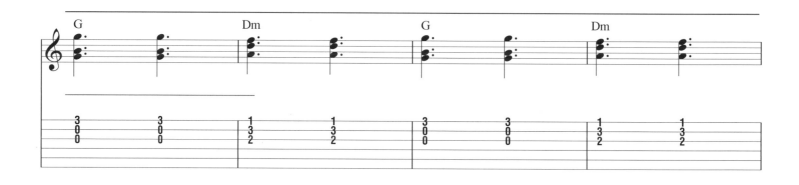

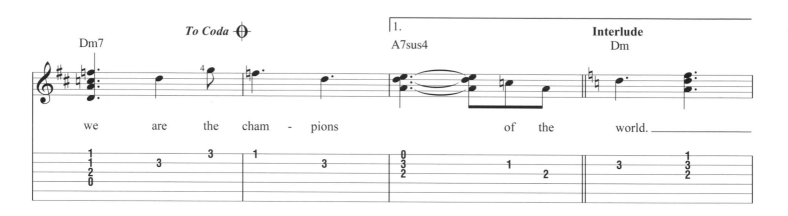

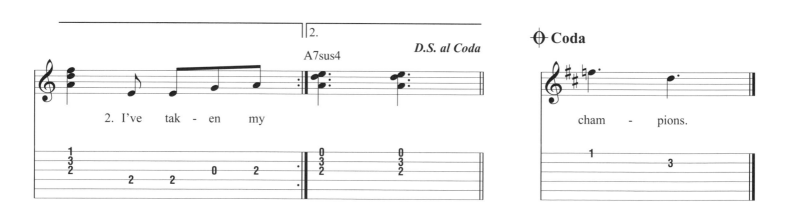

Additional Lyrics

2. I've taken my bows
   And my curtain calls.
   You brought me fame and fortune and ev'rything that goes with it.
   I thank you all.
   But it's been no bed of roses,
   No pleasure cruise.
   I consider it a challenge before the whole human race
   And I ain't gonna lose.

EASY GUITAR

WITH NOTES & TAB

This series features simplified arrangements with notes, tab, chord charts, and strum and pick patterns.

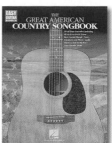  

MIXED FOLIOS

00702287	Acoustic	$19.99
00702002	Acoustic Rock Hits for Easy Guitar	$15.99
00702166	All-Time Best Guitar Collection	$19.99
00702232	Best Acoustic Songs for Easy Guitar	$16.99
00119835	Best Children's Songs	$16.99
00703055	The Big Book of Nursery Rhymes & Children's Songs	$16.99
00698978	Big Christmas Collection	$19.99
00702394	Bluegrass Songs for Easy Guitar	$15.99
00289632	Bohemian Rhapsody	$19.99
00703387	Celtic Classics	$16.99
00224808	Chart Hits of 2016-2017	$14.99
00267383	Chart Hits of 2017-2018	$14.99
00334293	Chart Hits of 2019-2020	$16.99
00403479	Chart Hits of 2021-2022	$16.99
00702149	Children's Christian Songbook	$9.99
00702028	Christmas Classics	$8.99
00101779	Christmas Guitar	$14.99
00702141	Classic Rock	$8.95
00159642	Classical Melodies	$12.99
00253933	Disney/Pixar's Coco	$16.99
00702203	CMT's 100 Greatest Country Songs	$34.99
00702283	The Contemporary Christian Collection	$16.99

00196954	Contemporary Disney	$19.99
00702239	Country Classics for Easy Guitar	$24.99
00702257	Easy Acoustic Guitar Songs	$17.99
00702041	Favorite Hymns for Easy Guitar	$12.99
00222701	Folk Pop Songs	$17.99
00126894	Frozen	$14.99
00333922	Frozen 2	$14.99
00702286	Glee	$16.99
00702160	The Great American Country Songbook	$19.99
00702148	Great American Gospel for Guitar	$14.99
00702050	Great Classical Themes for Easy Guitar	$9.99
00275088	The Greatest Showman	$17.99
00148030	Halloween Guitar Songs	$14.99
00702273	Irish Songs	$14.99
00192503	Jazz Classics for Easy Guitar	$16.99
00702275	Jazz Favorites for Easy Guitar	$17.99
00702274	Jazz Standards for Easy Guitar	$19.99
00702162	Jumbo Easy Guitar Songbook	$24.99
00232285	La La Land	$16.99
00702258	Legends of Rock	$14.99
00702189	MTV's 100 Greatest Pop Songs	$34.99
00702272	1950s Rock	$16.99
00702271	1960s Rock	$16.99
00702270	1970s Rock	$24.99
00702269	1980s Rock	$16.99

00702268	1990s Rock	$24.99
00369043	Rock Songs for Kids	$14.99
00109725	Once	$14.99
00702187	Selections from O Brother Where Art Thou?	$19.99
00702178	100 Songs for Kids	$16.99
00702515	Pirates of the Caribbean	$17.99
00702125	Praise and Worship for Guitar	$14.99
00287930	Songs from *A Star Is Born, The Greatest Showman, La La Land,* and More Movie Musicals	$16.99
00702285	Southern Rock Hits	$12.99
00156420	Star Wars Music	$16.99
00121535	30 Easy Celtic Guitar Solos	$16.99
00244654	Top Hits of 2017	$14.99
00283786	Top Hits of 2018	$14.99
00302269	Top Hits of 2019	$14.99
00355779	Top Hits of 2020	$14.99
00374083	Top Hits of 2021	$16.99
00702294	Top Worship Hits	$17.99
00702255	VH1's 100 Greatest Hard Rock Songs	$34.99
00702175	VH1's 100 Greatest Songs of Rock and Roll	$34.99
00702253	Wicked	$12.99

ARTIST COLLECTIONS

00702267	AC/DC for Easy Guitar	$16.99
00156221	Adele – 25	$16.99
00396889	Adele – 30	$19.99
00702040	Best of the Allman Brothers	$16.99
00702865	J.S. Bach for Easy Guitar	$15.99
00702169	Best of The Beach Boys	$16.99
00702292	The Beatles — 1	$22.99
00125796	Best of Chuck Berry	$16.99
00702201	The Essential Black Sabbath	$15.99
00702250	blink-182 — Greatest Hits	$17.99
02501615	Zac Brown Band — The Foundation	$17.99
02501621	Zac Brown Band — You Get What You Give	$16.99
00702043	Best of Johnny Cash	$17.99
00702090	Eric Clapton's Best	$16.99
00702086	Eric Clapton — from the Album Unplugged	$17.99
00702202	The Essential Eric Clapton	$17.99
00702053	Best of Patsy Cline	$17.99
00222697	Very Best of Coldplay – 2nd Edition	$17.99
00702229	The Very Best of Creedence Clearwater Revival	$16.99
00702145	Best of Jim Croce	$16.99
00702278	Crosby, Stills & Nash	$12.99
14042809	Bob Dylan	$15.99
00702276	Fleetwood Mac — Easy Guitar Collection	$17.99
00139462	The Very Best of Grateful Dead	$16.99
00702136	Best of Merle Haggard	$16.99
00702227	Jimi Hendrix — Smash Hits	$19.99
00702288	Best of Hillsong United	$12.99
00702236	Best of Antonio Carlos Jobim	$15.99

00702245	Elton John — Greatest Hits 1970–2002	$19.99
00129855	Jack Johnson	$17.99
00702204	Robert Johnson	$16.99
00702234	Selections from Toby Keith — 35 Biggest Hits	$12.95
00702003	Kiss	$16.99
00702216	Lynyrd Skynyrd	$17.99
00702182	The Essential Bob Marley	$16.99
00146081	Maroon 5	$14.99
00121925	Bruno Mars – Unorthodox Jukebox	$12.99
00702248	Paul McCartney — All the Best	$14.99
00125484	The Best of MercyMe	$12.99
00702209	Steve Miller Band — Young Hearts (Greatest Hits)	$12.95
00124167	Jason Mraz	$15.99
00702096	Best of Nirvana	$16.99
00702211	The Offspring — Greatest Hits	$17.99
00138026	One Direction	$17.99
00702030	Best of Roy Orbison	$17.99
00702144	Best of Ozzy Osbourne	$14.99
00702279	Tom Petty	$17.99
00102911	Pink Floyd	$17.99
00702139	Elvis Country Favorites	$19.99
00702293	The Very Best of Prince	$19.99
00699415	Best of Queen for Guitar	$16.99
00109279	Best of R.E.M.	$14.99
00702208	Red Hot Chili Peppers — Greatest Hits	$17.99
00198960	The Rolling Stones	$17.99
00174793	The Very Best of Santana	$16.99
00702196	Best of Bob Seger	$16.99
00146046	Ed Sheeran	$17.99

00702252	Frank Sinatra — Nothing But the Best	$12.99
00702010	Best of Rod Stewart	$17.99
00702049	Best of George Strait	$17.99
00702259	Taylor Swift for Easy Guitar	$15.99
00359800	Taylor Swift – Easy Guitar Anthology	$24.99
00702260	Taylor Swift — Fearless	$14.99
00139727	Taylor Swift — 1989	$19.99
00115960	Taylor Swift — Red	$16.99
00253667	Taylor Swift — Reputation	$17.99
00702290	Taylor Swift — Speak Now	$16.99
00232849	Chris Tomlin Collection – 2nd Edition	$14.99
00702226	Chris Tomlin — See the Morning	$12.95
00148643	Train	$14.99
00702427	U2 — 18 Singles	$19.99
00702108	Best of Stevie Ray Vaughan	$17.99
00279005	The Who	$14.99
00702123	Best of Hank Williams	$15.99
00194548	Best of John Williams	$14.99
00702228	Neil Young — Greatest Hits	$17.99
00119133	Neil Young — Harvest	$14.99

Prices, contents and availability subject to change without notice.

HAL•LEONARD®

Visit Hal Leonard online at **halleonard.com**

HAL·LEONARD GUITAR PLAY-ALONG

This series will help you play your favorite songs quickly and easily. Just follow the tab and listen to the audio to the hear how the guitar should sound, and then play along using the separate backing tracks. Audio files also include software to slow down the tempo without changing pitch. The melody and lyrics are included in the book so that you can sing or simply follow along.

INCLUDES TAB

Complete song lists available online.

VOL. 1 – ROCK	00699570 / $17.99
VOL. 2 – ACOUSTIC	00699569 / $16.99
VOL. 3 – HARD ROCK	00699573 / $17.99
VOL. 4 – POP/ROCK	00699571 / $16.99
VOL. 5 – THREE CHORD SONGS	00300985 / $16.99
VOL. 6 – '90S ROCK	00298615 / $16.99
VOL. 7 – BLUES	00699575 / $19.99
VOL. 8 – ROCK	00699585 / $16.99
VOL. 9 – EASY ACOUSTIC SONGS	00151708 / $16.99
VOL. 10 – ACOUSTIC	00699586 / $16.95
VOL. 11 – EARLY ROCK	00699579 / $15.99
VOL. 12 – ROCK POP	00291724 / $17.99
VOL. 14 – BLUES ROCK	00699582 / $16.99
VOL. 15 – R&B	00699583 / $17.99
VOL. 16 – JAZZ	00699584 / $16.99
VOL. 17 – COUNTRY	00699588 / $17.99
VOL. 18 – ACOUSTIC ROCK	00699577 / $15.95
VOL. 20 – ROCKABILLY	00699580 / $17.99
VOL. 21 – SANTANA	00174525 / $17.99
VOL. 22 – CHRISTMAS	00699600 / $15.99
VOL. 23 – SURF	00699635 / $17.99
VOL. 24 – ERIC CLAPTON	00699649 / $19.99
VOL. 25 – THE BEATLES	00198265 / $19.99
VOL. 26 – ELVIS PRESLEY	00699643 / $16.99
VOL. 27 – DAVID LEE ROTH	00699645 / $16.95
VOL. 28 – GREG KOCH	00699646 / $19.99
VOL. 29 – BOB SEGER	00699647 / $16.99
VOL. 30 – KISS	00699644 / $17.99
VOL. 32 – THE OFFSPRING	00699653 / $14.95
VOL. 33 – ACOUSTIC CLASSICS	00699656 / $19.99
VOL. 35 – HAIR METAL	00699660 / $17.99
VOL. 36 – SOUTHERN ROCK	00699661 / $19.99
VOL. 37 – ACOUSTIC UNPLUGGED	00699662 / $22.99
VOL. 38 – BLUES	00699663 / $17.99
VOL. 39 – '80s METAL	00699664 / $17.99
VOL. 40 – INCUBUS	00699668 / $17.95
VOL. 41 – ERIC CLAPTON	00699669 / $17.99
VOL. 42 – COVER BAND HITS	00211597 / $16.99
VOL. 43 – LYNYRD SKYNYRD	00699681 / $22.99
VOL. 44 – JAZZ GREATS	00699689 / $19.99
VOL. 45 – TV THEMES	00699718 / $14.95
VOL. 46 – MAINSTREAM ROCK	00699722 / $16.95
VOL. 47 – JIMI HENDRIX SMASH HITS	00699723 / $22.99
VOL. 48 – AEROSMITH CLASSICS	00699724 / $19.99
VOL. 49 – STEVIE RAY VAUGHAN	00699725 / $17.99
VOL. 50 – VAN HALEN: 1978-1984	00110269 / $19.99
VOL. 51 – ALTERNATIVE '90s	00699727 / $14.99
VOL. 52 – FUNK	00699728 / $15.99
VOL. 53 – DISCO	00699729 / $14.99
VOL. 54 – HEAVY METAL	00699730 / $17.99
VOL. 55 – POP METAL	00699731 / $14.95
VOL. 57 – GUNS 'N' ROSES	00159922 / $19.99
VOL. 58 – BLINK 182	00699772 / $17.99
VOL. 59 – CHET ATKINS	00702347 / $17.99
VOL. 60 – 3 DOORS DOWN	00699774 / $14.95
VOL. 62 – CHRISTMAS CAROLS	00699798 / $12.95
VOL. 63 – CREEDENCE CLEARWATER REVIVAL	00699802 / $17.99
VOL. 64 – ULTIMATE OZZY OSBOURNE	00699803 / $19.99
VOL. 66 – THE ROLLING STONES	00699807 / $19.99
VOL. 67 – BLACK SABBATH	00699808 / $17.99
VOL. 68 – PINK FLOYD – DARK SIDE OF THE MOON	00699809 / $17.99
VOL. 71 – CHRISTIAN ROCK	00699824 / $14.95

VOL. 74 – SIMPLE STRUMMING SONGS	00151706 / $19.99
VOL. 75 – TOM PETTY	00699882 / $19.99
VOL. 76 – COUNTRY HITS	00699884 / $16.99
VOL. 77 – BLUEGRASS	00699910 / $17.99
VOL. 78 – NIRVANA	00700132 / $17.99
VOL. 79 – NEIL YOUNG	00700133 / $24.99
VOL. 81 – ROCK ANTHOLOGY	00700176 / $22.99
VOL. 82 – EASY ROCK SONGS	00700177 / $17.99
VOL. 83 – SUBLIME	00369114 / $17.99
VOL. 84 – STEELY DAN	00700200 / $19.99
VOL. 85 – THE POLICE	00700269 / $17.99
VOL. 86 – BOSTON	00700465 / $19.99
VOL. 87 – ACOUSTIC WOMEN	00700763 / $14.99
VOL. 88 – GRUNGE	00700467 / $16.99
VOL. 89 – REGGAE	00700468 / $15.99
VOL. 90 – CLASSICAL POP	00700469 / $14.99
VOL. 91 – BLUES INSTRUMENTALS	00700505 / $19.99
VOL. 92 – EARLY ROCK INSTRUMENTALS	00700506 / $17.99
VOL. 93 – ROCK INSTRUMENTALS	00700507 / $17.99
VOL. 94 – SLOW BLUES	00700508 / $16.99
VOL. 95 – BLUES CLASSICS	00700509 / $15.99
VOL. 96 – BEST COUNTRY HITS	00211615 / $16.99
VOL. 97 – CHRISTMAS CLASSICS	00236542 / $14.99
VOL. 99 – ZZ TOP	00700762 / $17.99
VOL. 100 – B.B. KING	00700466 / $16.99
VOL. 101 – SONGS FOR BEGINNERS	00701917 / $14.99
VOL. 102 – CLASSIC PUNK	00700769 / $14.99
VOL. 104 – DUANE ALLMAN	00700846 / $22.99
VOL. 105 – LATIN	00700939 / $16.99
VOL. 106 – WEEZER	00700958 / $17.99
VOL. 107 – CREAM	00701069 / $17.99
VOL. 108 – THE WHO	00701053 / $17.99
VOL. 109 – STEVE MILLER	00701054 / $19.99
VOL. 110 – SLIDE GUITAR HITS	00701055 / $17.99
VOL. 111 – JOHN MELLENCAMP	00701056 / $14.99
VOL. 112 – QUEEN	00701052 / $16.99
VOL. 113 – JIM CROCE	00701058 / $19.99
VOL. 114 – BON JOVI	00701060 / $17.99
VOL. 115 – JOHNNY CASH	00701070 / $17.99
VOL. 116 – THE VENTURES	00701124 / $17.99
VOL. 117 – BRAD PAISLEY	00701224 / $16.99
VOL. 118 – ERIC JOHNSON	00701353 / $19.99
VOL. 119 – AC/DC CLASSICS	00701356 / $19.99
VOL. 120 – PROGRESSIVE ROCK	00701457 / $14.99
VOL. 121 – U2	00701508 / $17.99
VOL. 122 – CROSBY, STILLS & NASH	00701610 / $16.99
VOL. 123 – LENNON & McCARTNEY ACOUSTIC	00701614 / $16.99
VOL. 124 – SMOOTH JAZZ	00200664 / $17.99
VOL. 125 – JEFF BECK	00701687 / $19.99
VOL. 126 – BOB MARLEY	00701701 / $17.99
VOL. 127 – 1970s ROCK	00701739 / $17.99
VOL. 129 – MEGADETH	00701741 / $17.99
VOL. 130 – IRON MAIDEN	00701742 / $17.99
VOL. 131 – 1990s ROCK	00701743 / $14.99
VOL. 132 – COUNTRY ROCK	00701757 / $15.99
VOL. 133 – TAYLOR SWIFT	00701894 / $16.99
VOL. 135 – MINOR BLUES	00151350 / $17.99
VOL. 136 – GUITAR THEMES	00701922 / $14.99
VOL. 137 – IRISH TUNES	00701966 / $17.99
VOL. 138 – BLUEGRASS CLASSICS	00701967 / $17.99

VOL. 139 – GARY MOORE	00702370 / $17.99
VOL. 140 – MORE STEVIE RAY VAUGHAN	00702396 / $24.99
VOL. 141 – ACOUSTIC HITS	00702401 / $16.99
VOL. 142 – GEORGE HARRISON	00237697 / $17.99
VOL. 143 – SLASH	00702425 / $19.99
VOL. 144 – DJANGO REINHARDT	00702531 / $17.99
VOL. 145 – DEF LEPPARD	00702532 / $19.99
VOL. 146 – ROBERT JOHNSON	00702533 / $16.99
VOL. 147 – SIMON & GARFUNKEL	14041591 / $19.99
VOL. 148 – BOB DYLAN	14041592 / $17.99
VOL. 149 – AC/DC HITS	14041593 / $19.99
VOL. 150 – ZAKK WYLDE	02501717 / $19.99
VOL. 151 – J.S. BACH	02501730 / $16.99
VOL. 152 – JOE BONAMASSA	02501751 / $24.99
VOL. 153 – RED HOT CHILI PEPPERS	00702990 / $22.99
VOL. 155 – ERIC CLAPTON UNPLUGGED	00703085 / $17.99
VOL. 156 – SLAYER	00703770 / $19.99
VOL. 157 – FLEETWOOD MAC	00101382 / $17.99
VOL. 159 – WES MONTGOMERY	00102593 / $22.99
VOL. 160 – T-BONE WALKER	00102641 / $17.99
VOL. 161 – THE EAGLES ACOUSTIC	00102659 / $19.99
VOL. 162 – THE EAGLES HITS	00102667 / $19.99
VOL. 163 – PANTERA	00103036 / $19.99
VOL. 164 – VAN HALEN: 1986-1995	00110270 / $19.99
VOL. 165 – GREEN DAY	00210343 / $17.99
VOL. 166 – MODERN BLUES	00700764 / $16.99
VOL. 167 – DREAM THEATER	00111938 / $24.99
VOL. 168 – KISS	00113421 / $17.99
VOL. 169 – TAYLOR SWIFT	00115982 / $16.99
VOL. 170 – THREE DAYS GRACE	00117337 / $16.99
VOL. 171 – JAMES BROWN	00117420 / $16.99
VOL. 172 – THE DOOBIE BROTHERS	00119670 / $17.99
VOL. 173 – TRANS-SIBERIAN ORCHESTRA	00119907 / $19.99
VOL. 174 – SCORPIONS	00122119 / $19.99
VOL. 175 – MICHAEL SCHENKER	00122127 / $19.99
VOL. 176 – BLUES BREAKERS WITH JOHN MAYALL & ERIC CLAPTON	00122132 / $19.99
VOL. 177 – ALBERT KING	00123271 / $17.99
VOL. 178 – JASON MRAZ	00124165 / $17.99
VOL. 179 – RAMONES	00127073 / $17.99
VOL. 180 – BRUNO MARS	00129706 / $16.99
VOL. 181 – JACK JOHNSON	00129854 / $16.99
VOL. 182 – SOUNDGARDEN	00138161 / $17.99
VOL. 183 – BUDDY GUY	00138240 / $17.99
VOL. 184 – KENNY WAYNE SHEPHERD	00138258 / $17.99
VOL. 185 – JOE SATRIANI	00139457 / $19.99
VOL. 186 – GRATEFUL DEAD	00139459 / $17.99
VOL. 187 – JOHN DENVER	00140839 / $19.99
VOL. 188 – MÖTLEY CRÜE	00141145 / $19.99
VOL. 189 – JOHN MAYER	00144350 / $19.99
VOL. 190 – DEEP PURPLE	00146152 / $19.99
VOL. 191 – PINK FLOYD CLASSICS	00146164 / $17.99
VOL. 192 – JUDAS PRIEST	00151352 / $19.99
VOL. 193 – STEVE VAI	00156028 / $19.99
VOL. 194 – PEARL JAM	00157925 / $17.99
VOL. 195 – METALLICA: 1983-1988	00234291 / $22.99
VOL. 196 – METALLICA: 1991-2016	00234292 / $19.99

Prices, contents, and availability subject to change without notice.

0822
173